New
Frontiers
for
Business
Leadership

New Frontiers *for* Business Leadership

William C. Norris
Founder and Chairman, Control Data Corporation

DORN BOOKS
Minneapolis

Published by Dorn Books,
a division of Dorn Communications, Inc.,
7831 E. Bush Lake Rd., Minneapolis, MN 55435

First Edition

Book design by Sara Christensen

Printed in the United States of America

Library of Congress Catalog Card Number: 83-70908
ISBN 0-934070-21-0

Contents

Acknowledgements

This book is based on a number of papers dealing with Control Data Corporation's business strategy of addressing society's major unmet needs as profitable business opportunities. Over the past several years, I have spoken and written about the various programs Control Data has designed for this purpose, before many audiences at widely spaced intervals of time. Professor Harold F. Williamson, a distinguished business historian, undertook the task of fashioning this somewhat diverse array of material into the series of chapters which compose this book. I am indebted to him for the patience and skill with which he performed this not always easy task.

I am indebted also to Professor James C. Worthy, a member of our Board of Directors, for writing the Introduction, which provides a chronological and conceptual framework for the book as a whole.

Final editing and preparation of the manuscript for publication were the work of Ms. Pamela Espeland, on whose professional editorial judgment I came to rely.

Mr. Jerr Boschee, Director of Executive Office Communications, assisted in assembling materials for Professor Williamson and provided counsel on the organization and structure of the book. Ms. Mollie Price, Company Archivist, was most helpful in providing source documents and digging out and verifying factual materials. Mr. Eric Peper, Director of Control Data Business Centers, assisted in arranging for publication, and Ms. Kathryn Yates, Senior Consultant, Executive Office Communications, acted as liaison with the publisher supervising production of the book.

Above all, I am indebted to the many hard-working members of the Control Data organization whose imaginative insights and innovative thinking contributed so substantially to the evolution of the philosophy presented in this book, and whose dedicated efforts made it possible to convert this philosophy into operative reality. They not only helped formulate the ideas, but found the means to make them work. Other than Mr. Robert M. Price, President and Chief Operating Officer, and Mr. Norbert R. Berg, Deputy Chairman of the Board, to both of whom I am especially indebted, I cannot name here the many Control Data people who have contributed in one way or another to the programs I describe. If I go beyond these two top officers, I simply would not know where to stop; I am nevertheless grateful to each of them.

William C. Norris
Minneapolis, Minnesota
Spring, 1983

Editor's Preface

Control Data Corporation is a unique corporation, and William C. Norris, its founder, is a unique businessman. Not only has he fostered a number of highly innovative policies; he has also been willing and able to express publicly and in writing both what he is doing and the reasons behind his actions.

Over the past several years, Norris has delivered hundreds of addresses on Control Data programs to a variety of audiences. Taken together, they constitute a wideranging array of policy statements and represent a remarkable formulation of business philosophy. Many have previously been reprinted as pamphlets and given some circulation. But addresses are by nature a perishable art form, and what Norris has said and still has to say is too important to be allowed to sink into oblivion. At the urging of numerous people acquainted with his thinking, he agreed to the publication in book form of addresses he has given on various subjects.

Because the actual addresses were prepared for the particular times and occasions on which he spoke and aimed at particular audiences, and because he has spoken more than once on many of the topics selected, each chapter in this book is a synthesis of several different documents. Each chapter focuses on a specific area of concern: worker productivity and performance; education; urban revitalization; and so on. And each centers on Norris's business strategy of turning unmet needs into profitable business opportunities, a strategy that has undergirded Norris's business decisions since the beginnings of his career.

The task of editing Norris's addresses presented certain difficulties. Norris's thinking on various subjects is continually evolving and changing, as are Control Data's many programs. By the time this book appears in print, Norris will no doubt have further refined some of the thoughts here presented, and some of the Control Data programs here discussed will have taken new directions. Even so, Norris's thoughts and Control Data's programs are well worth recording and describing in their present form.

I am grateful to James C. Worthy for providing a detailed introduction that traces the development of Norris's thinking and business strategy over a period of some 40 years and serves as an overall framework into which the chapters can be placed. I am further indebted to him for the counsel and support he gave me during the editing process. Finally, I am indebted to Pamela Espeland for her valued assistance in the final preparation of the manuscript for publication.

Harold F. Williamson
Evanston, Illinois

Introduction

By James C. Worthy

William C. Norris is not only the founder of Control Data Corporation; he is one of the founders of the computer industry itself. He is the sole industry pioneer still active in the business and one of the very few still living.

Born in 1911 on a Nebraska farm, Norris showed an early bent toward the directions he would later take. As a boy, he built his own radio receiving and sending equipment and became an avid ham radio operator, acquiring along the way an abiding interest in the newly emerging field of electronics. His favorite high school course was physics, and he went on to study electrical engineering at the University of Nebraska. He was graduated in 1932, in the midst of the Great Depression; jobs were scarce, so he spent the next two years running the family farm for his recently widowed mother. In 1934 he was hired as a sales engineer at Westinghouse Electric Company, where he quickly demonstrated a flair for marketing which presaged much that would be central to his later life work.

Following the bombing of Pearl Harbor in 1941, Norris left Westinghouse to join the U.S. Naval Reserve. For reasons of which he was never quite sure, he was assigned to the Navy unit engaged in super-secret intelligence efforts: code-breaking, pinpointing enemy ship locations by intercepting high-frequency radio transmissions, and other activities requiring the rapid processing of vast streams of data. Even the most sophisticated high-speed mechanical devices then available were woefully inadequate, and Norris became involved in a group charged with designing and developing new electronic technologies that could be applied to intelligence problems.

He was deeply impressed by the men with whom he worked; in his words, the group was an "almost unbelievable assemblage of talent" that included mathematicians, engineers, and physicists from many leading universities and corporations, some of whom

11

already had international reputations. He learned to recognize and appreciate superior technical gifts, and he learned that creative people function best when they have ample resources to draw upon—lessons that would serve him well when he came to build his own organizations.

The urgent needs of all-out war had given powerful impetus to the swift evolution of new devices that were the forerunners of the digital computer. As the end of the war approached, it became obvious to those few in a position to know that the emergence of the digital computer would revolutionize computational technology and, by extension, cryptology. The Navy was deeply concerned about the impending dissolution of its prized intelligence unit; with demobilization, the men could no longer be kept in uniform, and few showed any interest in the civil service appointments they were offered. Thus, when Norris and some of his key associates proposed that they form a private company and continue working for the Navy, Secretary James V. Forrestal approved the plan as the only practical way to keep the team together.

In September of 1946, Engineering Research Associates, Inc. (ERA) was formed. Because the company had little capital, it brought in a group of outside investors headed by John E. Parker, an Annapolis graduate and successful investment banker with connections in both political and military circles. Ownership was divided equally between the insiders and the outsiders, with 100,000 shares sold to each group at ten cents per share to generate a total original equity of $20,000. Parker himself underwrote a $200,000 line of credit, and ERA opened for business in a former glider plant in St. Paul, Minnesota. The Navy promptly awarded the new company cost-plus-fixed-fee contracts to enable it to begin operations.

Parker was named president with responsibility for financial matters and overall management. Norris, one of three vice presidents, was originally in charge of marketing, but soon moved into operations as well. He recruited a qualified technical staff to supplement the founding core group, and ERA fast became known as a disciplined, cost- and schedule-conscious supplier of high-speed digital data-handling equipment and large-scale memories. Its principal customer was the Naval Computing Machine Laboratory, and though this meant that the company was somewhat hobbled by tight security, it also gave it the considerable advantage of working for a client with adequate financial resources and ready access to much of the advanced computer work going on elsewhere in government and private laboratories.

During its first year, ERA had revenues of $1.5 million and a profit of $34,000. It was still severely under-capitalized, but the Navy paid its bills promptly, and the company continued to grow. By 1951 the work force had expanded to around 1,500 employees, including many professionals and skilled technicians. ERA was now working for other federal agencies, including the Air Force and the Civil Aeronautics Administration, and its equipment had found its way into the BOMARC missile program—the predecessor of the SAGE continental defense system—and other advanced military applications.

As word of ERA's technical accomplishments began to spread beyond the confines of military security, elements of the infant private computer industry took notice. Among them was James Rand of Remington-Rand. He was one of the first businessmen to sense the commercial possibilities of electronic computers, and soon after World War II ended he had established the Norwalk, Connecticut, Laboratory. In 1950 Remington-Rand had acquired the Eckert-Mauchly Computer Corporation, a small company which had originally developed for the Army equipment that was used to calculate artillery trajectories. In the fall of 1951, Rand approached Parker with the intent of acquiring ERA.

Uncomfortably aware of ERA's always tenuous financial position, Parker was receptive to Rand's overtures and, after hard bargaining, sold the company for approximately 85 times what the original founders had paid to start it only five years before. Norris, who was then vice president and general manager, was opposed to the sale, as were his fellow insiders. There was little they could do about it, however, since Parker had the financial control, and they reluctantly agreed to go along with his decision.

Parker took his handsome profit and turned to other interests; Norris and his colleagues remained in St. Paul, where Remington-Rand had agreed to let the company stay.

With the acquisition of ERA, Remington-Rand had assembled the strongest array of technical computer talent in the world. IBM, Burroughs, National Cash Register, and others all had nascent capabilities, but none had the technical resources to match the organization James Rand had put together. Unfortunately, Remington-Rand's managerial capacities were not equal to Rand's strategic foresight. Its three computer units—ERA, Eckert-Mauchly, and the Norwalk Laboratory—reported to different corporate departments and operated as fiercely independent entities. Left largely to their own devices, the individual operating units accomplished important breakthroughs. The Eckert-Mauchly group produced the Univac system that successfully predicted the outcome of the 1952 presidential election; Univacs I and II, which were installed in the U.S. Census Bureau, greatly speeded the tabulation of the 1950 census of population and the 1954 census of business. The ERA group made the fastest and most reliable hardware in the industry and pioneered the introduction of transistors to replace the bulky, failure-prone vacuum tubes which had been basic to computer electronics. Despite these and other important technical achievements, both Eckert-Mauchly and ERA suffered from the lack of central direction and coordination from Remington-Rand.

ERA's operations were further hampered by the fact that much of its work was so secret that its nature could not be disclosed even to corporate headquarters. When at one point ERA obtained the Navy's permission to bring out a civilian version of a high-speed computer originally developed for the military, corporate officers were amazed to learn some of the things that had been going on and how far the state-of-the-art had progressed. This particular piece of equipment formed the basis for ERA's first major venture into the nonmilitary market; the hardware which stemmed from it was able to process great masses of data at a speed, cost, and level of reliability unprecedented in the civilian market.

In 1955, Remington-Rand and Sperry Corporation merged to form Sperry-Rand. The new company consolidated the several disparate computer units under the Univac name and made Norris vice president and general manager of computer operations. Sperry-Rand was now a unified computer business entity incorporating research, engineering, manufacturing, and marketing capabilities under strong centralized leadership. The future looked promising.

Norris urged Sperry-Rand to take the substantial resources it had assembled and use them to become the world's principal supplier of computers. Under the elder Thomas Watson, IBM had been mesmerized by the success of its tabulating machines and slow to grasp the significance of the new electronic technology. The younger Thomas Watson, who had taken over in 1946, was determined to move his company into the computer age, but the way was still clear as late as the mid-1950s for Univac to become what IBM in fact became. Sperry-Rand let its chance slip by, hesitant to make the investments and take the risks Norris knew were necessary. Meanwhile, IBM forged ahead, and by the late 1950s it had become the dominant factor in the new industry, a position it holds to this day.

"We sat there," Norris recalls, "with a tremendous technological and sales lead and watched IBM pass us as if we were standing still." Finally, the frustration proved too much to bear. In the summer of 1957, Norris and eight of his key associates walked out and formed Control Data Corporation.

The new corporation was financed initially by the sale of 600,000 shares of common stock at $1 per share. It ushered in the dollar stock era in the United States and was the first computer company to be publicly financed. There were some 300 stockholders, and none held a controlling interest; with the ERA experience still fresh in his mind, Norris was determined that no one—not even he—would ever be in a position to sell the company over the objections of the other owners. Shares were purchased by members of the founding group, by their friends, and by scattered investors intrigued by the glamour of the emerging computer industry.

Norris and the eight engineers who had followed him set up shop in rented quarters in an old warehouse across the street from the Minneapolis Star and Tribune Company. In the ensuing months, they were joined by other disaffected Univac engineers. Floor space was divided by temporary chipboard partitions, which five years later were still standing and still unpainted. In this unpretentious setting, Norris and his colleagues determined to design and manufacture the world's largest and most powerful solid-state transistorized computers.

By that time IBM dominated the industry, and other major companies were struggling to find a place for themselves. IBM's greatest strength lay in business data processing, which was then thought to represent 80 percent of the total potential market. Its rivals directed their efforts toward the same market segments, but this proved to be a costly strategy that resulted in head-to-head confrontations with the giant. Many of IBM's most financially sound competitors—notably General Electric, RCA, and Bendix—eventually withdrew in defeat.

Control Data was a very small fish in a sea of very big predators, but that did not worry Norris because he had picked a different place to swim. With financial resources of less than two-thirds of a million dollars, he and his associates chose to stake out their position in an area where their special technical and professional expertise would give them a decisive advantage: large-scale computers for engineering and scientific applications. IBM and others were also interested in exploring this area, but none as yet had the technological skills to match those of the group Norris had assembled.

Fully transistorized, Control Data's computers incorporated the most advanced elements of electronic technology. Initially, they were sold with little accompanying software to customers who could write their own programs and did not need the kind of hand-holding that novice users required. Clients like the Atomic Energy

Commission and the Defense Department were soon joined by some of the nation's largest universities, including Illinois, Wisconsin, and Michigan State, who appreciated the new equipment's unique problem-solving capabilities.

Even though Control Data had the field virtually to itself, at least at the outset, its strategy of concentrating on giant computers was fraught with risk. Simply learning how to build such computers was a chancy undertaking because state-of-the-art technology—by definition new and untried—carries with it not only the hope of success but the danger of failure. The potential market for the type of computer Control Data produced was limited to federal government laboratories, a handful of universities, and a relatively small number of corporations engaged in military and atomic energy research and development. The company's precarious financial position meant that a minor error in judgment or a stroke of bad luck could have been fatal, and its sole reliance for revenues on a narrow product line posed another hazard. IBM, National Cash Register, Burroughs, Honeywell, RCA, General Electric, and Bendix all had substantial earnings from other well-established products and services; if the going in the new field proved too rough, they could always fall back on other resources. Control Data had to make it with its big computers, or not make it at all.

The strategy came perilously close to failing. In the beginning, about all the new company had was brains. Among other things, it was sorely lacking in manufacturing facilities, and it especially needed metalworking and related machinery. Realizing that Control Data would have to expand quickly if it were going to stay alive, Norris embarked on an aggressive acquisition program.

In 1958, Control Data acquired Cedar Engineering, Inc., a Minneapolis manufacturer of aircraft instruments. This not only provided production facilities, but also furnished a line of revenue-generating products. The acquisition soaked up a sizable part of the company's meager reserve of working capital, but the financial crisis was resolved when Allstate Insurance Company purchased a $350,000 issue of six percent preferred stock.

Control Data had to make it with its big computers, or not make it at all.

Subsequent acquisitions were made primarily for the purpose of obtaining needed technologies. Control Corporation (acquired in 1960) brought with it desirable know-how in gas, oil, and water distribution control systems; Holley (in 1961) added capabilities in the design and manufacture of printers; Meiscon (in 1963) afforded competence in engineering design; and the computer division of Bendix (also in 1963) resulted in an influx of skilled personnel. These and other moves greatly broadened and strengthened Control Data's technical competence.

It is important to note that all of the acquisitions were friendly and none was a forced takeover. In most instances, the acquired company was in trouble and seeking a buyer who would pay the best price for its skills, product lines, and markets, and use them most effectively. For many technically sound smaller companies, Control Data was the preferred buyer.

Acquisitions were accomplished by the exchange of stock. After emerging from its early difficult years, Control Data became for a while one of Wall Street's favorite glamour issues. In the "go-go period" of the 1960s, investors were entranced with almost anything electronic, and Control Data's stock was bid up to heights that gave the company considerable leverage in exchange-of-stock transactions and allowed it to make a number of desirable acquisitions on very favorable terms. The most striking of these was the acquisition of Commercial Credit Company in 1968.

Since the day of its founding, Control Data had been plagued by a chronic shortage of cash, and its rapid growth had placed a severe strain on its limited resources. In addition, many computer systems were leased rather than sold outright, and the debt that was incurred to finance the lease build-up had an unfavorable impact on the company's balance sheet. During the latter part of the 1960s, Control Data prepared a ten-year projection of the financing it would need to cover equipment on lease; the figure came to an astounding $1 billion—higher, a company insider joked, than anyone at Control Data could count. This amount was obviously one that could not be obtained by conventional means. A possible answer lay in the acquisition of a finance company whose ability to leverage its debt could be used to advantage.

It happened that Commercial Credit of Baltimore was at that time actively looking for a buyer. A diversified financial-services company with $3.4 billion in working assets, it was the object of a hostile takeover effort and wanted to find an acquirer in whom its management could have confidence. Cognizant of Control Data's lease-financing problems, it made overtures to which Control Data eagerly responded. A deal satisfactory to both parties was swiftly worked out, and in August of 1968 Commercial Credit became a wholly owned subsidiary of Control Data Corporation.

The merger proved highly beneficial to all concerned. Under Norris's leadership, and with the cooperation of Commercial Credit's management, a remarkable degree of synergism developed between the two companies, which could hardly have been more dissimilar in their traditions and technologies. Commercial Credit retained its corporate autonomy and its own board of directors, which was necessary for legal reasons and enabled it to preserve its credibility in the financial community. Control Data had found a solution to its leasing dilemma; at last it had sufficient means to finance this crucial part of its business. This would not be the only advantage Control Data realized from the acquisition: between 1968 and 1980, Commercial Credit would contribute nearly $550 million in profits to its parent and pay another $150 million in dividends. Today both companies are stronger than either could have become without the other.

Well before the acquisition of Commercial Credit Company, Control Data had successfully accomplished two significant strategic moves: entry into the peripheral products business, and entry into data services. Each made a tremendous difference in the company's subsequent viability and growth.

While Control Data had originally directed its efforts toward a relatively small and specialized segment of the computer mainframe market, it soon became clear that this market alone was not enough to support the technical and manufacturing resources that went along with it. Moreover, the giant computer market is inherently volatile: large expenditures such as those required to purchase Control Data computer systems are among the most readily postponable items in military, scientific, and university budgets. Control Data was well established in the scientific computer sector, but it needed to build a broader and more stable customer base.

As much as two-thirds of the total cost of a data processing system is represented by peripheral equipment: tape and card readers, magnetic tape transports, random access memories, high-speed printers, and the like. Without the support of peripherals equal to its demands, the central processing unit—the heart of the system—is helpless. The computers Control Data was building necessitated peripherals with extraordinary performance capability and reliability; since these were not available from other companies, Control Data had no choice but to design and build its own. Unfortunately, high-speed peripherals are expensive to develop, and economies of scale are extremely important in their manufacture. Norris therefore decided on a bold course: Control Data would develop and make peripherals for *other* computer firms as well as for itself. At that time IBM was the only company that could supply its own peripherals, and there were several other companies in the same position as Control Data. These, Norris argued, would be prime prospects for Control Data products should the company venture into original equipment manufacture, or OEM.

"If we don't, someone else will," Norris contended. Still, he was strongly opposed by some of his key people, and there were those close to him who objected bitterly to giving their competitors the benefits of their own technical advances. Norris ultimately prevailed, but at the loss of at least one long-time valued associate.

The decision to move into the OEM market proved to be a sound one. Other computer manufacturers welcomed Control Data as a new source of high-quality, reasonably priced equipment for their own products. In 1969-71, when the bottom temporarily dropped out of the giant computer market, Control Data would be able to weather the storm largely because of its OEM business.

Part of Control Data's OEM strategy involved joint ventures with other computer manufacturers. In the mid-1960s, for example, Norris proposed to National Cash Register that they embark on a cooperative undertaking; the two companies had been good customers for each other's products since the early 1960s. After protracted discussions and negotiations, a deal was finally consummated in 1972. The result was the formation of the jointly owned Computer Peripherals, Inc. (CPI) to manufacture high-speed printers, magnetic tape systems, disk memories, and related products, initially for the two parent companies and later for a broader market.

At about the same time Control Data began moving into peripheral products, Norris was envisioning yet another potential market: data services. There were many companies both large and small which were technically sophisticated enough to use big computers; few of them, however, could invest in the type of equipment Control Data offered or keep the equipment busy enough to make it cost-effective. Control Data's computers were simply too powerful and too expensive to have wide appeal. Thus Norris decided, in his words, to "sell a little piece of a big computer at a time." If a customer needed only a few minutes or an hour of computer time each day, Control Data would make a computer available for that period and charge accordingly.

It was a revolutionary concept, and, like Norris's decision to manufacture and sell peripherals to other companies, it was met with considerable internal resistance. It was also met with external skepticism; Wall Street thought that Control Data should stick to what it did best—building equipment—rather than venturing into a new and risky market. IBM had already made a tentative foray into data services and had achieved indifferent success; how could Control Data expect to do better?

Once again, Norris prevailed. In accordance with his plan to make the power of big computers "available to the guy who couldn't afford to invest in one," Control Data opened its first data service center in Minneapolis in 1962 with a computer that was being used by the company for test purposes. In time, more centers were added, and all were eventually linked together in a nationwide and then worldwide network called CYBERNET.

At first the data services offered consisted of nothing more than "raw time" on a big computer. Before long, however, Norris and his associates realized that another lucrative market could be tapped if Control Data also furnished specialized software that would address individual industries and specific user needs. In the years that followed, the company worked in close cooperation with users to develop a sizable volume of software in such areas as seismic exploration and engineering design. The process was time-consuming and costly, but the long-term payoff was substantial.

Control Data's services business was given a powerful boost in 1973 with the resolution of an antitrust suit the company had filed against IBM five years earlier. Control Data was then an upstart new company that was establishing a foothold in the market for large-scale computers. In an effort to prevent Control Data from preempting the field, IBM embarked on a crash program to overtake it and adopted selling techniques which Norris considered unfair, unethical, and illegal. Angered and embittered, he fought back.

The suit was supported by an imposing catalog of damning complaints and demanded triple damages for the losses inflicted on Control Data by IBM's alleged illegal actions. It also called for the dismemberment of the offending giant—an audacious touch.

During the discovery proceedings, Control Data's attorneys examined over 28 million pages of IBM documents, photocopied one million pages, and added over 500,000 pages—about 150,000 documents—to its own already formidable computerized data base. Had the company not been in possession of a powerful computer and the sophisticated software needed to perform the tasks of indexing, sorting, retrieving, and summarizing, it would not have been possible to effectively utilize this enormous quantity of information. The suit was one of the first occasions on which high-speed computer technology was used in a major legal proceeding. It not only affected the final outcome of the suit, but also created a new revenue-producing data service that was subsequently provided for a fee to other parties involved in large, complex legal actions.

At the outset, Control Data's decision to take on IBM in what was bound to be a lengthy legal confrontation seemed foolhardy in the extreme. Wall Street, the legal fraternity, and the general business community openly questioned Norris's judgment. One observer echoed the feelings of many when he said, "Bill Norris has lost his marbles." To inquiries from worried friends, Norris responded that he knew what he was doing. As it turned out, he certainly did: IBM paid a heavy price to get Control Data off its back. The settlement included $101 million in cash, a capital infusion Control Data sorely needed. It also allowed Control Data to acquire IBM's data services subsidiary, the Service Bureau Company, on attractive terms.

The acquisition of the Service Bureau Company was important to Control Data for three reasons. First, it more than tripled Control Data's service business. Second, it greatly broadened its service market; up until then, Control Data's services had been oriented primarily to engineering and scientific applications, and the Service Bureau Company added a strong business data processing orientation supported by a diverse and well-knit software base and an established market. Third, the acquisition brought with it a first-rate management staff; as Norris would comment with satisfaction some years later, "they were really loaded with talent." A further feature of the settlement was a stipulation that IBM stay out of data services for six years, a period Control Data used to good advantage to consolidate its position.

Ironically, the acquisition of the IBM-equipped Service Bureau Company made Control Data at that time one of the largest single commercial users of IBM equipment. The Service Bureau Company was integrated with CYBERNET into a highly efficient and profitable network of data processing services. With 50 CYBERNET centers operating on six continents, Control Data now enjoys an exceptionally strong position in the international data services market.

In the twenty-five years from 1957 to 1982, Control

Data grew under Norris's guidance from a minuscule operation with $600,000 in assets to a corporation with assets of $6.9 billion; from eight employees to over 56,000; from zero revenues to $4.3 billion. Net profits rose from a negative number to $155 million.

A breakdown by business segments is even more revealing of the shrewdness of Norris's entrepreneurial strategy. During the latter half of the 1970s, the peripherals business grew at a 31 percent compound annual rate, data services at a 19 percent rate, and computer systems at a respectable but modest seven percent rate. In 1982, revenues from computer systems totaled $705 million compared with $1 billion *each* for the once untried, unfamiliar, and, to some of Norris's associates, unwanted peripherals and services.

Control Data now holds a commanding worldwide lead in both peripherals and services, continues to produce the most powerful computer systems in the world, and, through Commercial Credit, is one of the United States' premier financial institutions. It is altogether an impressive record for a company that started out a little over two decades ago with less than two-thirds of a million dollars and a handful of engineers without much going for them but exceptional technical capabilities and a strong, imaginative leader.

At the root of Control Data's phenomenal success is Norris's business strategy: identifying unmet needs and turning them into profitable business opportunities. He began by perceiving the emerging need of the engineering and scientific community for powerful computers to perform large and complex computations that had never before been attempted—and often not even conceived—simply because the machines capable of handling them had not yet been invented. He then moved to address the needs of the computer industry for peripherals that were too costly for most individual manufacturers to design and produce for themselves. He turned next to the needs of smaller clients who could not afford to own computers but would benefit from using them for limited periods of time. In each instance, the need existed, but the market did not; it had to be created.

Markets were created in all three areas by recognizing and defining the needs, designing means for approaching them as profit-making enterprises, and bringing the two together. Basic to this process was new product development. Also basic to it was the understanding that quick payouts were not to be expected. Control Data did not pay its first dividend until its 20th year of operation; during those two decades, the company was profitable in all but two brief periods, but every dollar earned was plowed back into the business.

Norris recognizes that it takes time and commitment to create new markets. Under his direction, Control Data has always exhibited a marked willingness to seek out new areas of opportunity, to take risks, and to stick with new ventures through thick and thin. In an era when too much emphasis is placed on short-term earnings and not enough on innovation and ingenuity, Norris is perceived as something of a maverick. But even his harshest critics cannot argue with his success.

In the words of Robert M. Price, Control Data's president and chief operating officer, "Bill Norris has more insight and foresight than anyone I've ever known. Some who do not know him well think of him as a wild visionary. But that's wrong. He simply sees the potential of things before others do. And he knows what a great advantage it is to be first in a new field." As it turned out, some of those new fields proved quite surprising.

During Control Data's early years, Norris appeared to take little interest in social issues. The interest may well have been there, but the demands of the struggling company took precedence and were the focus of most of his thoughts and actions. In 1967, however, two critical events took place that would result in his leading Control Data into radical new frontiers of corporate strategy and public policy.

In 1967, Norris attended a seminar for chief executive officers at which Whitney Young, then head of the National Urban League, led a discussion on the social and economic injustices to which blacks in America were continually subjected. It opened Norris's eyes to disturbing vistas of American life. Not long afterward, Minneapolis and St. Paul were torn by race riots.

Local leaders were appalled. This was the sort of thing that happened elsewhere, *not* in the Twin Cities! Civic groups gathered to debate the whys and wherefores and to suggest various courses of action that might prevent such events from occurring in the future. Considerable funds were raised to ameliorate some of the more obvious affronts to middle- and upper-class conceptions of social dignity.

Meanwhile, Norris took decisive steps on his own. One of the things he had learned from Whitney Young was that jobs were critically important. He called his key people together and announced that Control Data would have to do better at hiring blacks than it had done in the past. "Unless these young blacks have jobs," he told them, "until they have something to look forward to and work for, we're going to have trouble in Minneapolis and everywhere else." He stressed that he was not just talking about civic duty, as so many others were. "My God," he said, "you can't do business in a society that's burning!"

Control Data had long adhered to a policy of non-discrimination in its hiring practices. But few blacks had actually been hired, primarily because all of the company's Twin Cities plants were located on the periphery of the metropolitan area and were often inaccessible by public transportation from the inner city, where most blacks lived. Norris appointed a small task force under Norbert R. Berg, then personnel vice president and now deputy chairman of the board, and instructed it to find ways to break down the barriers. After careful study, the task force returned with its conclusions: before it could hire significant numbers of blacks, Control Data would have to put a plant in the inner city. "Fine," Norris responded. "Make it a new one."

Norris insisted on a new plant because he wanted the people in the community to know that Control Data's intentions were serious. Once the commitment had been made, there would be no turning back. To ensure that this would be the case, Norris also insisted that the plant be given responsibility for manufacturing a product essential to Control Data's business. At that time, the company was in need of additional manufacturing capacity in several areas, including peripheral controllers—a vital component of any computer system and especially critical to Control Data's giant computers. Workers in the new north Minneapolis plant would make peripheral controllers. This would not be merely another low-skilled tent-making operation, as one prominent company had set up in the Watts area of Los Angeles following the riots there.

Both of Norris's decisions flew in the face of conventional wisdom. There was obviously a sizable inner-city labor pool on which to draw, but would Control Data find quality as well as quantity? Assuming that a competent work force could be built, wouldn't the task present far more difficulties than the company had encountered in opening any of its other plants? And rather than putting the plant in charge of a crucial product, wouldn't it be better to plan on hiring mostly low-skilled workers and letting them manufacture a product that wasn't too important to the business? What if the plant failed, or its output was not up to standard?

"If you leave room for failure," Norris has often said, "you're very likely to fail." He deliberately created a situation in which retreat was out of the question. It is well that he did, for there were many times when those in charge of bringing the plant on line and delivering a quality product would have called the whole thing off if they could have. Instead, they were forced to find solutions to problems as they arose.

When it opened in 1968, it was understood that the Northside plant, as it was called, would be brought up to the same levels of production, quality, and cost performance as its sister plants elsewhere. While it took somewhat longer to accomplish this goal—approximately three years rather than the usual one—it was accomplished, and today Northside is one of the most efficient plants in the entire Control Data system.

Northside provided jobs for people seeking full-time employment, but it did not address the needs of those who were able to work only part time. Within the inner-city community were many mothers with school-age children who could work only during school hours, and high school, trade school, and college students who could work only during nonschool hours. In 1970, Control Data opened its Selby plant in St. Paul. It currently employs several hundred mothers and students in three four-hour shifts.

Control Data's two original inner-city ventures were milestones in the development of the company. The Northside undertaking has since been replicated in other disadvantaged areas across the country, including a town in southern Appalachia that bears the dubious distinction of being in the poorest county in the contiguous 48 states. Plants modeled on the Selby concept are going up in other cities as components of larger urban revitalization efforts.

Norris and his associates learned a great deal from both the Northside and Selby experiences. They learned that it was possible—not easy, but possible—to build a competent, motivated work force with people who had been considered unemployable. They learned that assisting employees with their off-hour problems made them more productive in the workplace. They learned that plants that offered a few hundred steady jobs could significantly upgrade the quality of life in individual neighborhoods and go a long way toward stabilizing communities. These lessons made a lasting impression on Norris. From 1968 on, the conviction that jobs are central to solving a wide range of social problems has been a ruling force in his thinking and has played a major role in the shaping of his business policies.

Many of the practices that were introduced to deal with the special problems of the Northside and Selby employee populations were subsequently found to be useful in other company operations as well. Skills acquired in counseling employees with pressing job, home, and personal problems evolved into the Employee Advisory Resource program, or EAR, a company-wide counseling service. Exposure to the human and economic costs of poor employee health habits marked the beginning of an interest in employee health that later flowered into the ambitious StayWell program. Experience gained from supervising women and minority workers in the inner-city plants proved valuable in training managers and executives throughout the company.

A number of the programs originally developed to meet the needs of inner-city plants have also been found to be salable outside the company. What was learned from converting the hard-core unemployed into productive workers became the basis of the Fair Break program, which is now operating on contract with a variety of public and private agencies across the country. Among the subscribers to EAR is a professional athletics league, whose member clubs have found the service to be of value to their stress-prone players. StayWell is offered at an attractive per capita rate to other companies concerned about employee health.

It is important to realize that Norris's decisions to commit Control Data to the Northside and Selby plants and the myriad programs that stemmed from them were not contrary to his original business strategy of identifying unmet needs and turning them into profitable business opportunities. Instead, they were reasonable and logical extensions of that strategy. True, the unmet needs were of a social rather than a business or technical nature—unlike the needs for big computers, for example, or peripherals—but they nevertheless embodied tremendous potential as business enterprises. None of these undertakings has ever been viewed as charitable endeavor.

It costs more time and money to bring facilities such as Northside up to fully efficient levels of production than it does to make more traditional plants work. It also costs time and money to initiate and implement programs such as EAR and StayWell. In Norris's eyes, however, these represent good R&D investments. And, as good R&D investments are apt to do, they have paid off by laying the groundwork for a series of new businesses which hold great promise for the future.

At about the same time the Northside and Selby plants were becoming operational, another major Control Data project was approaching maturity. This was the PLATO computer-based education and training system, a highly sophisticated and uniquely successful application of computer technology to the teaching and learning process.

The idea for what would become the PLATO system

originated at the University of Illinois Champaign-Urbana campus in 1959, when Dr. Donald Bitzer of the university's Coordinated Science Laboratory was given the assignment of finding a way to use the computer for instructional purposes. With two assistants—a programmer and a technician—Bitzer set about ingeniously rigging together various pieces of equipment gathered from around the laboratory. In only a few weeks, he had created a terminal capable of interacting with a central computer and, with the aid of suitable software, performing instructional functions. The initial machine, software, and courseware were crude by later standards, but they demonstrated the practicability of the basic concept.

More developmental work was begun, Bitzer's staff grew rapidly, and the laboratory's total needs soon exceeded the capacities of its existing computer facility. The pioneering but aging ILLIAC I, designed during the 1940s by University of Illinois scientists, was also used heavily by researchers in other branches of the university, and there was simply not enough computer time to go around. The laboratory secured funding and purchased one of Control Data's new large-scale computers for its exclusive use. The equipment was operational by 1961, but by then it had become obvious that Bitzer's group needed its own computer.

Norris, following events from Minneapolis, was intrigued from the outset with the PLATO project. During his Navy days, and later at ERA, he had wondered whether it might be possible to speed up and improve the quality of training methods by using digital computers. The idea had been theoretically sound, but impractical from the standpoint of cost. Computer technologies had been vastly improved since then, however, and costs had sharply declined, and now Bitzer was demonstrating—on Control Data equipment—that computers could be effectively utilized for training and education purposes. Through his staff, Norris watched Bitzer's progress closely, and by 1965 he was ready to make an offer to help Bitzer meet his insatiable appetite for computer time.

Norris proposed that Control Data install one of its most powerful computers rent-free at the University of Il-

The initial machine, software, and courseware were crude by later standards, but they demonstrated the practicability of the basic concept.

linois for the exclusive use of the PLATO unit. If the university agreed to share information on the PLATO project and its technology with Control Data, the only costs it would have to bear would be those of insurance and maintenance. An agreement was reached, signaling the beginning of one of the most fruitful collaborative efforts in the history of academic-corporate relationships.

In the early days of the joint endeavor, the National Science Foundation contributed valued support, but the primary responsibility for furnishing financial and other resources was assumed by the university and Control Data working in cooperation. Over the years, Control Data has not only provided successively more powerful computers and substantial funding, but has also participated in designing and perfecting ways of turning PLATO into a marketable commodity. A great deal of time and money were required to make the system fully operational; although it was clear from 1967 on that the concept was viable, it was not until 1975 that PLATO had reached the point where it could be offered as a service on a commercial basis. Since then, Control Data has borne all of the considerable costs of moving the technology into the marketplace.

As the problems of Northside and other Control Data inner-city plants were brought under control, Norris began looking around, in his words, for "other fires to put out." He did not have far to look. One of the greatest difficulties Control Data had encountered in making the plants operational was that of training employees who had been poorly educated. As Norris surveyed the national scene, he could not help but notice that the quality of public education had been steadily deteriorating over the years. He saw in PLATO the means for dealing effectively with this grave social need, and in 1976 the system was made available for adoption by schools.

By and large, the proffered technology has been greeted with indifference and even resistance. While the extent of its use has been growing gradually, it is still far short of what it should be; this is evident from the fact that where the system has been adopted, the results have been spectacular. Norris is confident that more educators, administrators, school boards, and government agencies will eventually recognize PLATO's potential.

Meanwhile, other applications are being developed and implemented. A growing number of corporations in the United States and abroad are turning to PLATO for industrial training. Control Data itself is the single largest user of PLATO and attributes to it much of the credit for its own high level of employee productivity. Through Control Data Institutes, Learning Centers, Business Centers, and Business and Technology Centers located in the United States and around the world, PLATO is bringing instructional services to hundreds of organizations and tens of thousands of individuals. The system also plays a large part in other Control Data programs both within and without the company.

Since Control Data first embarked on the PLATO program in conjunction with the University of Illinois some 18 years ago, it has spent an estimated $900 million on the project. Part of this amount has been devoted to enhancing the technical capabilities of the system, but most of it has gone into building the vast body of courseware necessary to support a comprehensive education system, and into creating and administering the far-flung distribution network necessary to undergird PLATO's large-scale use.

So far as can be determined by conventional accounting procedures, PLATO has yet to show a profit. However, according to Robert M. Price, the real figures are hard to determine. Control Data's system of internal record-keeping is remarkably efficient, and the revenues and costs directly related to PLATO are easy to ascertain, but many of the benefits of the system are indirect and difficult or impossible to include in accounting statements. As Price points out, PLATO is "so pervasive through all our service businesses that it is going to be very hard to actually add up all the dollars that are flowing from it." He emphasizes that PLATO's value to the company goes far beyond the income it generates from outside education and training applications. Not only has it resulted in a multitude of technology spinoffs; its effects have been felt throughout the entire corporation.

Norris remains convinced that Control Data's investment in PLATO will eventually prove worthwhile in the marketplace as well. Much of the nation's school system is on the verge of bankruptcy, and the quality of education is declining as school boards try desperately to make ends meet. While the costs of labor-intensive conventional education are rising, however, the costs of capital-intensive PLATO are steadily falling and will continue to fall as technologies become more advanced. Although PLATO is considerably more expensive and complex than hand-held calculators, what has happened in recent years to the price of those devices is illustrative of what is happening now with computer systems. New markets are continually developing in such fields as military education, proprietary education, and other settings largely independent of the educational establishment, but Norris is sure that the greatest potential market exists in mainline education. One day, he feels, PLATO will be the most prolific revenue generator of all of Control Data's many businesses. True to form, he is willing to wait.

From the time of the 1967 riots onward, Norris has been deeply concerned with the issue of job creation. The lack of enough jobs to go around is one of America's major unmet needs, and Norris believes that the proper use of new and emerging technologies can go a long way toward alleviating it. Over the years, Control Data has provided thousands of new jobs by pursuing technologies that have formed the bases for new products, new services, and new businesses.

To Norris, technology is not necessarily technical. He prefers to define it simply as "know-how," or the ability to make something or do something. Thus defined, technology includes not only complex mechanisms and devices, but also the understanding, skill, and imagination that go into their development and production. In any event, technology does not stand alone: it must be accompanied by the innovation required to generate it and the entrepreneurship required to use it.

Although we live in what is termed a big business economy and huge organizations dominate the national scene, small business is the source of most innovative ideas and entrepreneurial efforts and a major source of new technology. It also accounts for the majority of the new job formation in the United States, despite its high mortality rate and various impediments to its progress.

Norris came out of a small-business background to build Control Data; ERA was a small company prior to its acquisition by Remington-Rand. Control Data itself was a small enterprise during its formative years. Thus Norris understands both the workings and the needs of small business. In the early 1970s, realizing the critical role that small business plays in new job creation, he arrived at the conclusion that the most effective way to address the country's pressing need for jobs was to strengthen small business and foster the formation and profitable growth of new small enterprises. He began viewing small business as a market with unmet needs that Control Data was uniquely equipped to serve.

Many companies offer products and services which are utilized by small enterprises, and many products and services are designed with small business in mind. But no one before had visualized small business in and of itself as an identifiable and potentially lucrative market. Fully convinced that it was, Norris set about reorienting Control Data and its constituent entities to provide a broad spectrum of services aimed especially at that market.

His efforts were greatly aided by the presence of Commercial Credit Company, which Control Data had acquired in 1968. Commercial Credit had brought with it nearly 1,000 field offices through which it furnished a wide range of financial services complementary to Control Data's computer services and capable of being marketed with them. Many of Commercial Credit's customers were small companies, and when Norris's small-business strategy began to take form some four or five years following the acquisition, he had a ready-made customer base on which to build. This base was further augmented by the acquisition of IBM's Service Bureau Company in 1973.

In the latter part of the 1970s, Control Data began offering a variety of services tailored to the special needs of small business for technology, training, personnel recruitment, and consulting. Technotec and Worldtech were developed to facilitate the process of technology exchange in the interests of encouraging both innovation and entrepreneurship. New courseware and software were designed for the PLATO system to meet the training needs of small business. CYBERSEARCH, an electronic employment service, was created to help small businesses recruit competent personnel for engineering, data processing, and sales positions. Control Data Temporary Personnel Services—or Control Data Temps—was formed to provide a convenient, efficient, and cost-effective way for small enterprises to fill their short-term requirements for professional, technical, office, and light assembly workers. More recently, Business Advisors, Inc. (BAI), a wholly owned subsidiary, was organized for the purpose of supplying high-quality management-consulting services responsive to the needs and characteristics of small business.

As these and other new services added significantly to Control Data's abilities to aid the small-business sector of the economy, it became apparent that new means of delivery would be necessary to make them more readily available to larger numbers of users. A network of Control Data Business Centers and Business and Technology Centers (BTCs) was established to serve as the core of a sophisticated delivery system. The Business Centers are, in effect, retail stores in which small-business owners may examine an array of services and select the ones they most need. The BTCs are large buildings or clusters of buildings in which space is leased to small enterprises; Control Data's various services are then offered on site. Both the Business Centers and the BTCs are relatively new, and only a few are currently in operation, but nationwide chains of both are being deployed.

Norris's approach to the small-business market has followed a by now familiar pattern. He began by identifying a need that was not being adequately met: specifically, the need for more accessible and affordable services that would help existing small businesses and stimulate the launching of new ones. He then proceeded to re-orient some of the services Control Data already offered and to design a number of applicable new ones. Finally, he set about bringing the need and the services together to create a market.

As has been the case so often in Control Data's history, the decision to enter this market embodied a high degree of risk, and it will take time before it proves profitable to the company. But Norris is confident that the market will eventually be a large one and well worth the investment required to establish it.

Norris places great store in cooperative undertakings and has long advocated their usefulness. Under his guidance, Control Data has entered into a number of joint ventures with other companies, including the formation of Computer Peripherals, Inc. in conjunction with National Cash Register in 1972. The PLATO system was the result of a successful cooperative venture between Control Data and the University of Illinois. Countless other examples could be cited to illustrate Norris's belief that pooling technologies and sharing resources can be beneficial to all concerned.

In 1978, Control Data embarked on a totally new type of cooperative undertaking: City Venture Corporation, a consortium of business, professional, and religious entities. It has as its goal nothing less than the revitalization and renewal of run-down urban areas.

City Venture stemmed in part from Control Data's experiences with the Northside plant. To make that facility operational, management had to learn—often by trial and error—to deal not only with unforeseen problems at the work site, but also with numerous difficulties which had their origins in conditions that existed outside the plant. Some proved to be quite beyond the scope of Control Data's expertise and abilities. Many employees recruited for the new plant were impoverished and poorly educated. Housing in the community was severely deteriorated, and even workers who found steady jobs at Northside had trouble securing decent places for their families to live.

Thirteen years after the Northside plant opened, conditions in the surrounding area were pretty much as they had been after the debris from the riots and fires had been cleared away. No other large employers had followed Control Data into that part of Minneapolis, and little in the way of new small-business activity had emerged. Although Control Data's plant had unquestionably made an important contribution to the well-being of at least a portion of the population, it remained an island in an otherwise depressed area. It simply lacked the "critical mass" necessary to achieve the self-sustaining reaction capable of revitalizing the area as a whole.

Norris and his associates came to realize that three basic elements are absolutely essential to the successful revitalization of a community: jobs, education, and housing. Providing those elements is a task of enormous magnitude and complexity. To Norris, it represents a unique and stimulating challenge—and a tremendous business opportunity. In his words, "the building and rebuilding of our cities affords an opportunity to establish a new growth industry potentially at least as important as the automobile in the earlier years of this century."

City Venture is the vehicle that has been fashioned to seize this opportunity. It markets its services—which include the initiation, planning, and management of comprehensive urban renewal programs—to communities, cities, states, and federal agencies. Thus far, it has achieved significant results in Toledo and the Park Heights area of Baltimore and has contracted with several other cities around the country.

In 1979, Control Data entered into another cooperative undertaking that is modeled closely on City Venture in terms of its organization and basic purpose. But while City Venture focuses on the problems of the larger cities, the newer consortium, Rural Ventures, is aimed at revitalizing small-scale agriculture.

Although Norris has spent most of his adult life in cities, he has never pulled wholly free from his family farm origins. He has a strong philosophic commitment to small-scale farming that is much like his commitment to small-scale business. In fact, he views the small farm as simply a special form of small business that is capable of creating new jobs not only for the farm family, but also through the various support services required for a thriving farm community. In an era when large-scale farming appears to be well on its way to dominating the American agricultural scene, Norris is convinced that the application of new and emerging technologies can make small farms viable once more and re-establish them as vital cultural and economic resources. He believes that information technology in particular can be adapted to the special needs of the small farmer, and a large portion of Rural Ventures' efforts have gone toward formulating an extensive data base and providing access to appropriate technologies and PLATO courses through Agricultural Business and Service Centers (ABCs).

Like City Venture, Rural Ventures was formed in recognition of an unmet need and serves that need in various ways. It will doubtless open up a new market of major proportions, and that market will not be confined to the United States. By far the greatest opportunity for improving small-scale agriculture is found in the developing countries of the world. A necessary pre-condition for the industrialization most of these countries are now trying desperately to achieve is an agricultural base capable of supporting an industrial non-food-producing population without which industrial development is impossible. The investment Control Data is currently making in nurturing small-scale agricultural technology in the United States in effect represents an investment in R&D which has vast potential not only in business terms, but also in terms of human welfare on an international scale.

Both City Venture and Rural Ventures rely heavily on government participation at the local, state, and federal levels. This is true of a number of other Control Data programs as well. Government participation is something Norris has long been accustomed to and comfortable with. Unlike many businessmen today, who typically display visceral anti-government and pro-free-enterprise biases, Norris not only accepts the notion of government involvement in a variety of matters which directly touch upon the daily lives of ordinary citizens; he also believes that government should in some cases be *more* involved than it is and actively solicits that involvement. At the same time, he feels that there are situations in which business and government work best alone. There are some things that business can do better than government, and it should be allowed to do them; there are other things that can be dealt with only by government, if at all, since they are quite beyond the capacity of business to accomplish. To address the most critical areas of unmet needs, however, Norris advocates as the optimum approach a cooperative arrangement between business and government into which each can bring its own unique resources and abilities.

Norris's business success has always depended on substantial government participation. ERA was put together to serve the ongoing needs of the Navy and other government agencies for powerful electronic data processing equipment, and its revenues were largely drawn from public sources. From its beginnings, Control Data's most important single customer for computer equipment has been the U.S. government.

When he began looking for ways to expand his business activities into the arena of social needs, Norris had no qualms about the prospect of government involvement. With City Venture, Rural Ventures, and other socially responsive programs, he is simply continuing a practice he has followed all of his business life.

The story of Control Data is one of constantly expanding business horizons. Beginning with a very narrow product line of powerful computers and a limited customer base, the company soon branched into the design and production of peripheral equipment for other computer manufacturers, and then into the selling of computer time to clients who could not afford giant computers of their own. Within a decade of its founding, Control Data had moved from a highly specialized enterprise to a broadly based one. Under Norris's leadership, it grew by creating markets where none had existed before.

In arriving at the conclusion that many of our society's most serious unmet needs could be addressed as business opportunities, Norris's course of thinking did not differ materially from the manner in which he had earlier come to see the business opportunities inherent in giant computers, peripheral products, and data services. From his perspective, social problems merely represent different kinds of unmet needs. Admittedly, they are far more complex than technical problems, and effective solutions are far more difficult to find and implement; this is due in part to the fact that large numbers of people and organizations are likely to be involved in the process and their interests will often conflict. Unmet social needs must perforce be approached differently than unmet technical needs; they take longer to satisfy, and the criteria for judging the efficacy of their solutions are far more ambiguous. When has an unmet need been met, and who is to make that determination? These are troublesome questions.

Furthermore, "technical" and "social" are not necessarily dichotomous. Many social problems have been created by technology, but developments in technology have simultaneously made it feasible for the first time to solve many social problems. Information technology embodies especially promising possibilities, and it is in this area that Control Data's greatest strengths lie.

Norris has identified an interesting array of unmet social needs which he believes can be converted into profitable business opportunities. These and the ways in which he has chosen to deal with them make up the substance of this book. For now, it is sufficient to emphasize that the underlying strategy he uses to approach these new areas of opportunity is not that different from the one he employed to bring Control Data into more technical markets. In systematically addressing unmet social needs as business opportunities, Norris is simply moving into a new phase of broadening and strengthening Control Data's business base. He is confident that these developing markets will in time exceed both in scope and profitability any of the other markets the company has thus far entered. It may be as much as ten years or even longer before some of them reach fruition, but Norris and his associates have learned that these things take time. In terms of strategic directions, the company is well positioned for the next quarter century.

Norris's business strategies have evolved within an overall conceptual and attitudinal framework. The processes by means of which various elements of these strategies developed were not always as neat and orderly as they might appear from the formulation given here, however. According to Norbert R. Berg, who has worked closely with Norris for many years and is familiar with his ways, "Many times [Norris] gets his strategic directions from his gut. He gets a feeling that this is the way we've got to go, and then it's amazing how he can elicit from people building blocks that make sense. . . . He just starts you with the end point and then makes you sweat to get there. It's an interesting form of genius." Norris himself says, "It is very hard to know what will work and what won't. Strategy is something that evolves in your mind, and you suddenly figure, 'This is what I'm going to do.' "

Although Norris's strategic thinking is not systematic in the textbook sense of the word, it is characterized by three discernible traits. First, he always has a sense of direction. Second, he is able to visualize relationships between resources and opportunities that are not always readily apparent. Third, he has the capacity to learn from experience. Each major undertaking he has initiated has stemmed from something that has gone before, and each new advance in Control Data's business has opened up new possibilities.

Often, the initial move into what became an important new entrepreneurial field was at the outset nothing more than an action which was required to implement a previous decision. The company moved into peripherals to make its big-computer strategy work. It originally entered into data services merely to sell computer time; only later did it become apparent that value could be added to that time in the form of special user-oriented software, which has since become the heart of the data services business. The experiences acquired in making the Northside plant successful were subsequently utilized in numerous other applications. In short, Norris and his associates have developed a remarkable knack for doing what needs to be done to carry out a prior decision and then looking around for other ways to use what they have learned and accomplished.

Needless to say, not all of the ideas for developing new businesses originate with Norris. Many of them in fact do, but not the least of his achievements has been the creation of a management staff that is sensitive to unmet needs—technical, social, and otherwise—and has the imagination to see how they can be converted into business opportunities. He is ably assisted by a highly motivated group of executives who not only are stimulated by the challenge of turning his ideas into realities, but are capable of generating ideas of their own.

Norris also enjoys the confidence and support of a strong board of directors. Control Data's directors have minds of their own and often call on management to justify proposed courses of action. By the same token, they have learned to respect Norris's business judgment because it has proved consistently sound over a long period.

There is no Bill Norris waiting in the wings to succeed Bill Norris; he is a unique individual, and it would be a mistake to try to find a duplicate. Within Control Data's top management group, however, are people who have been thoroughly schooled in Norris's thinking and clearly understand the strategic directions he has laid down. Norris has provided well for Control Data's future.

Most businesses today are not concerned with social needs except as objects of charity. To Norris, this perspective is sorely lacking in two important respects; it neglects the substantial business opportunities that reside in unmet social needs, and it evinces business's unwillingness to assume what he feels is its responsibility to society.

Meeting social needs has traditionally been considered the province of institutions other than business: governments, churches, private charities, and the like. But with its vast stores of under-utilized technologies and other resources, business—to a degree not true of these other institutions—is uniquely equipped to take the initiative in planning and implementing the large-scale programs necessary to effect significant changes. The prominent position business occupies within our economy and our culture carries with it a large degree of responsibility; in Norris's eyes, this requires far more in response than the occasional or even regular charitable gift or undertaking. What it requires, in short, is that businesses find ways to integrate the meeting of social needs into the vital processes of their enterprises.

Norris is not opposed to "good works"; he recognizes that charity plays a vital role in our society. He is, however, much opposed to equating responsible corporate behavior with good works. Activities undertaken on a charitable basis tend to be fair-weather efforts that are subsequently curtailed or dropped with the onset of economic difficulties. In contrast, activities undertaken as an integral part of the business itself, which business comes to depend on for revenues and profits, are far more likely to survive periods of adversity.

Control Data's experience in moving aggressively to address a wide range of unmet social needs is the subject matter of this book. What Norris has to say deserves to be studied with care as a record of the thinking of a business leader who has greatly broadened the concept of the role of business in American life and redefined the character and magnitude of corporate social responsibility.

PART ONE

1

Social Needs and Business Opportunities

Inflation, unemployment, and underemployment are among the most serious ills which have combined to erode the quality of life for many in Western society, where large numbers of poorly educated, disabled, and disadvantaged individuals are denied the opportunity to be more productive and are frustrated in their efforts to attain more meaningful levels of existence. The situation is far worse for the majority of those who occupy the other three-quarters of the globe and have yet to achieve an even minimally acceptable standard of living. The gap between the rich and poor nations continues to grow as developing countries attempt to cope with widespread illiteracy, malnutrition, inadequate health care, and a lack of job opportunities for their expanding populations. Rich and poor nations alike are burdened with the economic problems brought on by the decline in the availability of cheap energy, the degradation of the environment, limited supplies of natural resources, and lagging creativity and innovation.

Government has traditionally been held responsible for solving such problems. The fact that conditions have become steadily worse over the years, however, makes it clear that government has failed in this role and that fundamental changes are needed in the way we address society's major needs.

One key change is for business to take the initiative and provide the leadership in planning, managing, and implementing programs designed to meet society's needs and turn them into business opportunities. Along the way, business must cooperate with government, labor unions, universities, organized religion, and other influential segments of society. Where the resources of a single com-

SOURCE
"Evaluation of the Best Business Strategy in the World" address, 1980-81 Distinguished Lecture Series, Laboratory for Computer Sciences, Massachusetts Institute of Technology, Cambridge, Massachusetts, February 19, 1981.

Inflation, unemployment, and underemployment are among the most serious ills which have combined to erode the quality of life for many.... Large numbers of poorly educated, disabled, and disadvantaged individuals are denied the opportunity to be more productive.

pany are insufficient, as will often be the case, two or more companies should work together on joint projects or ventures. In any event, there should be an appropriate sharing of costs between business and government.

It was our growing conviction that business could and should assume a leadership role that prompted Control Data to adopt such a strategy in the late 1960s. We have pursued it vigorously and with sound results ever since. In general, the reaction of the business community has been to view us as both unrealistic and idealistic and to assume that our "grand social experiment" will ultimately prove unsuccessful at the expense of our stockholders. At the same time, many persons in government and other sectors have welcomed the possibility of business as an ally while timidly withholding their full support, ostensibly awaiting more evidence of the strategy's effectiveness.

This reluctance may be attributed to a lack of understanding of our social and economic system and an unwillingness to recognize how serious and deep-seated its problems are. The typical business executive, for example, does not appreciate how pivotal technology has been to our economic growth and development and how its application can contribute to alleviating or solving our problems. Most legislators either share this misunderstanding or do not have the courage to propose laws that would inevitably require sacrifices. The man on the street knows even less about technology and its relationship to jobs and other aspects of our quality of life. Yet our society is increasingly dependent on technology.

It is left to the business community to take a more innovative stance, and this necessitates a significant shift in attitude. At the present time, most large corporations, with their vast resources and established markets, generally prefer to boost profits by improving existing products and services. They may acquire other products and services by absorbing small companies, but this is not the same as creating something themselves.

The failure of business to be more innovative is largely a function of our increasingly no-risk culture. Innovation means doing something original, often at great expense—first with regard to development, and later in the initial manufacturing and marketing stages. The rising costs of innovation, combined with pressure from investors for immediate earnings and the uncertainty caused by an unstable economy, have resulted in a tendency on the part of corporations to avoid the risks associated with truly innovative actions. The emphasis instead is on realizing instant payoffs by marginally upgrading current offerings and by lowering labor costs through mechanization and automation. In this type of environment, the development of new products and services—and therefore new jobs—is relegated to a back seat.

The reluctance to take risks is not confined to the business community. The education establishment is resistant to the changes brought on by declining student populations, escalating costs, and its own all too apparent inability to meet individual needs. Universities are no longer in the vanguard in many scientific, economic, and social fields. Labor unions shun cooperation with corporations in addressing the needs of society—and, by extension, of their own members. Foundations give money out of their income to alleviate social ills, but they put virtually none of their assets into high-risk investments. Most religious organizations are reactionary, having a penchant to criticize without offering realistic solutions to problems and remaining on the sidelines when it comes to confronting major social issues.

While business continues to follow a policy of maximizing short-term gains with minimum risk, there are signs that it is beginning to recognize that it has responsibilities beyond just making a profit. These are commonly termed "social responsibilities," and they encompass a wide range of activities. Their main focus is on non-shareholder constituencies: employees, customers, suppliers, and communities.

When a business becomes conscious of its social responsibilities and willing to do something about them, it starts looking for ways to maximize its positive effect on its non-shareholder constituencies while minimizing its negative impact. Usually the business turns to such policies and programs as equal job opportunities for employees, improved career counseling for the disadvantaged, counseling for chemically dependent workers, community involvement, heightened product safety, pollution reduction, energy conservation, charitable contributions, and the like. These and other approaches are receiving increased emphasis of late, largely because experience has shown that the failure to address social problems can be very costly in terms of labor efficiency and product quality. In other words, for a business to heed and act upon its social responsibilities is not mere altruism; rather, it reflects enlightened self-interest and good business sense.

Each corporation has its own views as to what its social responsibilities are and how they should be met. Most opt for one or more of the actions cited above. But even though these efforts are all highly laudable, their end results tend to be narrow in scope and small in scale. Meanwhile, major societal needs are left relatively unattended. And these are the needs that underlie and are inter-related with inflation, unemployment, underemployment, and similar woes.

That these problems persist only serves to underscore the fact that corporations must effect fundamental changes in their strategy. They must begin turning unmet social and economic needs into profitable business opportunities, with the costs being shared between themselves and government. This strategy should be widely adopted, and I believe it will be someday, because it will come to be seen as the appropriate course of action for the Prudent Man.

Throughout business history, the Prudent Man has set an important example and provided business with invaluable guidelines. At present, however, he is an ostrich with his head in the sand, hiding from the tough realities of an increasingly complex world. He is long overdue to lift his head and look around him, for society's major unmet needs are crying for his attention—and presenting him with unique opportunities.

The strategy of addressing social needs from a business perspective is not new to the Prudent Man. But he seems to have forgotten what he learned early in this century from Henry Ford and other entrepreneurs, and it is time for him to review the facts.

When Henry Ford realized that a growing rural America urgently needed better transportation, he responded by building a great corporation. Hundreds of thousands of jobs were created in its factories and related service businesses; untold numbers of people made fortunes on the Tin Lizzy. General Wood of Sears, Roebuck founded a highly profitable network of retail stores to serve the diversifying needs of a new American middle class. Westinghouse and General Electric both flourished as they served the nation's burgeoning needs for electrical power. Countless other examples from the past could be mentioned here, but I believe that these serve to illustrate my point: history teaches that addressing major unmet social needs is sound business.

Granted, things are different today. Society's needs are more complex, and responding to them effectively often requires that large quantities of resources be amassed through cooperative arrangements. For various reasons, though, most corporations are unable to contemplate such an approach, let alone adopt it. They are hindered by the arrogance inherent in large corporations, by the desire for autonomy, by bureaucratic inertia, and by their own distaste for collaboration. In addition, the traditionally adversarial relationship between business and government prevents them from seeing the potential of those alliances.

The unwillingness to cooperate with others is aggravated by the fact that most executives have a somewhat narrow field of interest. They are inordinately influenced by stockholder pressures to deliver short-term earnings, and they are overly concerned with the executive bonuses geared to the current year's bottom line. They do not choose to see beyond these boundaries because the risk is too great. If they adopted a more creative or innovative strategy—one which embodied a commitment to social needs—then the adequate return on their investments would come much later than the majority of investors and corporate managements prefer.

In reality, however, business can ill afford not to play a more active role in solving society's problems. The high expectations built into our culture—in large part a result of the achievements of business—together with the persistence of crime, poverty, illiteracy, unemployment, and the inequality of opportunity, put a heavy financial burden on business. They even jeopardize the survival of business as we know it.

One of the primary tasks of management is to foresee dangers and take steps aimed at avoiding or dealing with them. The health and vitality of an enterprise requires that threats be identified far enough in advance for appropriate action to be initiated. Management has an obligation to do what it can to correct or relieve conditions inimical to the long-term viability of the enterprise and of the environment upon which it depends. The environment presents opportunities as well as threats, and threats can sometimes be converted to opportunities. Some of the most serious threats, in fact, have the potential for becoming the greatest business opportunities. To turn one's back on the environment—to go about one's business while ignoring social needs—is to allow threats to go unchecked and opportunities to pass one by.

There are many reasons why big business can and must take the initiative in addressing society's major unmet needs. The main reason is that no other sector of society has such capabilities for effectively planning, assembling the resources for, and managing the large and diverse programs necessary today. Most government agencies are focused on single fields—labor, commerce, housing, agriculture, or urban development—and lack both the competence and the authority to confront social problems that require multifaceted solutions. This is equally true of education, foundations, and other non-profit institutions. On the other hand, these organizations can make essential contributions to broad-scale programs out of their own expertise and authority. The key, once again, is cooperation.

It is especially important that government participate financially in any endeavor of this type. By this I do not mean to imply that our government should invest heavily in private business, or that federal budgets should be increased solely for the purpose of financing industrial research and development. I do feel, however, that government funding would be highly appropriate for planning, research, special facilities, education, and training during the initial stages of a program while its validity is being tested and proved.

But even if government funding were made available for these purposes, it would not be enough in itself to attract the needed corporate commitment, given the long-term payout typical of such ventures and the current emphasis on improvements in short-term earnings. In order to get corporations involved, legislation must be enacted to provide them with financial incentives, possibly in the form of tax credits. These tax credits might be offered to corporations which form consortia to address major social needs, devote some of their resources to urban and rural revitalization, spin off under-utilized technology for use by small businesses, and/or invest in seed capital companies to finance the start-up of small firms undertaking high-risk technological innovations.

Investors—especially institutional investors—can play a crucial role in this process by encouraging corporate management to view unmet social needs as business opportunities. The guidelines given investment managers should be modified in such a way as to remove some of the restrictions which now inhibit investment in projects with long-term payouts.

Foundations should be more open to the idea of working with business. Today, any meaningful association with a for-profit endeavor is anathema to most foundations. They feel that an involvement of this type would threaten their non-profit status, or they find profit-seeking enterprises somehow distasteful, or they worry that cooperating with business will tarnish their image of impeccable integrity and lofty ideals. As a consequence, most foundation-sponsored projects are too small and address only the symptoms, not the root causes, of major social problems, and the benefits they yield are temporary. More lasting results would almost certainly be obtained if foundations were to pool their enormous resources with those of business.

It seems reasonable that foundations could allot a minimum of ten percent of their investable funds to companies with a strategy of addressing major social needs. I am convinced that this could be done without exceeding the bounds of tolerable risk, and that the level of such investments could logically be increased over time. Religious organizations could follow similar practices in the management of their own investment portfolios.

Education should heed its responsibility to stimulate innovative responses to the needs of society. Business schools could be at the forefront of constructive change by adapting their curricula to teach a method of strategic planning based on social need, as opposed to the present unimaginative and nearly universal practice of applying a strictly return-on-investment approach. Even labor unions—although this might be too much to hope for—could adopt an attitude of greater receptivity to measures designed to improve worker productivity; this would be a great boon to the economy and to the workers themselves.

Government, foundations, religious organizations, the education establishment, and labor unions: all must become more active in addressing society's major needs. But the main thrust must come from business. In this regard, let me re-emphasize that a strategy aimed at meeting social needs should not be perceived as something separate from or in addition to the traditional course of business. Instead, it should be seen as an essential part of management's obligation to maintain the health and continued economic viability of the enterprise. In our increasingly complex society, unmet social needs present business with a wealth of potentially profitable and enduring opportunities. Recognizing them as such—and acting upon them—should eventually come to be regarded as normal business procedure. So should large-scale cooperation with government and other sectors, since this is the only way to make the fullest use of existing resources.

The strategy I have been outlining here is one Control Data has followed for years. In spite of the many discouraging experiences I have had while promoting it, I sense that a change is taking place in the climate of business opinion. More business leaders seem aware that responding to unmet social needs makes good business sense, and more seem willing to consider participating in consortium-type approaches to some of the problems that stand in the way of the American dream.

Business cannot do the job alone, but without active business involvement the job cannot be done at all. Granted, there are a number of barriers, psychological and otherwise, that now inhibit the exercise of creative business leadership. I believe that these can be surmounted, however, and I also believe that the most effective means of doing this is by demonstrating success on a substantial scale, as Control Data has been doing. The strategy has worked for us; there is no reason why it cannot work for others as well.

2

Technological Cooperation for Survival

From the very beginnings of mankind, technology has shaped human destiny. Not only has it been basic to the emergence and survival of the species, it has also enabled man to master his environment and subdue nature, to conquer space and time, to create beautiful structures, and to relieve his mind and muscles of onerous burdens. Unfortunately, technology has frequently been hindered by widely varying perceptions and misperceptions of what it is and does.

Too often technology is equated with anything big—business, government, universities, industry—and with the harmful effects that these are assumed to have on people's lives and on the environment. In reality, however, technology has and can be used both for good and ill, both to make life easier and to destroy it, both to tame hostile nature and to jeopardize its delicate balance.

In ancient times the use of fire and the domestication of

SOURCES

"Technological Cooperation for Survival" address (also published as part of a technology booklet series), Institute of Electrical Engineers, London, England, February 25, 1977.

"A Policy for Export of Products & Technology" address (also published as part of a technology booklet series), Fifteenth Goddard Memorial Symposium of the American Astronautical Society, Washington, D.C., April 1, 1977.

"Better Management of Technology" address, Medtronic, Inc., Minneapolis, Minnesota, November 27, 1978.

"A Businessman's Perspective on the Transborder Data Flow Issue" address, International Conference on Transnational Data Flow, New York, New York, November 28, 1978.

"Urban and Agricultural Problems" address, Congressional Symposium, Minneapolis, Minnesota, May 4, 1979.

"Optimizing World Technological Resources for Mankind" address (also published as part of a technology booklet series), World Computing Services Industry Congress, San Francisco, California, June 24, 1980; to the European Management Forum, Davos, Switzerland, February 5, 1980; and at a conference sponsored by the University of Wisconsin, Milwaukee, Wisconsin, November 8, 1979.

plants and animals greatly enhanced man's ability to feed and clothe himself. Later, irrigation and other forms of water management were key to the establishment of advanced civilizations in Mesopotamia and along the Nile. The use of these technologies also engendered massive and sometimes detrimental changes in the environment. In Mesopotamia, unwise irrigation practices eventually ruined the topsoil; in the Middle East and elsewhere, the overgrazing of arid land turned untold millions of previously productive acres into useless desert.

It does not follow, though, that the introduction of new technologies will invariably bring about adverse side effects or that society cannot take the steps necessary to remedy or control them—or, with foresight, prevent them. For example, the invention of the automobile gave the American public a low-cost, highly convenient mode of transportation. It also resulted in large numbers of accident-related injuries and deaths and increased air pollution. Rather than allowing these problems to go unchecked, society installed traffic lights, licensed drivers, imposed speed limits, improved highway construction, and equipped cars with emission-controlling devices. Similar arguments can be posed for many other new technologies: their use may have brought about unforeseen and unfortunate consequences, but in general man has been able to handle them.

There is no doubt that technology is vital to our existence. The question is one of where we should go from here. Looking at what man has done in the past with his hands, mind, and tools, I am convinced that technology can in the future be utilized to alleviate or eliminate our major social and economic problems, and that we have both the will and the ability to deal with any undesirable side effects. In order for technology to reach its maximum effectiveness, however, we must change the ways in which we perceive, apply, and disseminate it.

Technology has been somewhat formally defined as industrial science or the systematic knowledge of the industrial arts. I prefer to define it simply as "know-how"—as a way of doing things and organizing actions to achieve desired results. This "know-how" has been combined with the physical sciences to achieve such diverse results as steam transportation, the internal combustion engine, iron and steel production, the generation of electricity, and hybrid corn. But technology is not confined to the application of the physical sciences; there are also important technologies based on the social sciences. These are used to organize factories, manage businesses, handle labor relations, establish educational systems, and operate government bureaucracies. Most practical technologies embody elements from both sciences. The telephone is a good example: while it was derived from the physical sciences, strategies for its application came out of the social sciences.

In other words, technology embraces and permeates all aspects of our lives. It is the lifeblood of our society—the process, the "know-how," that creates new products and services and improves existing ones. And it is the single most important source of new jobs.

Technology is critical to human and economic progress. Economically advanced and developing countries alike urgently need improved agricultural and industrial production; better education; adequate health care; increased employment; and abundant, affordable sources of energy. These needs will go unmet unless there is a worldwide acceleration of technological innovation. This in turn cannot be achieved without more efficient utilization of existing technology, more development of new technology, and, above all, more technological cooperation.

One of the world's largest untapped resources is the wealth of information and technology lying dormant or under-utilized in the libraries and laboratories of businesses, governments, research institutes, academic institutions, and individual inventors. Thus far, the transfer of information and technology between industries, from government to business (and vice versa), and among small and large businesses has been carried out with dismal inefficiency. As a result, we are wasting some of our greatest assets. Time and again, official studies have shown that major innovations occur when technologies developed in one industry are applied to problem-solving in another.

Control Data's Techno-van provides on-site demonstrations of Technotec, Control Data's technology transfer service.

These studies have also shown that small companies are better innovators in many respects than large companies.

Most small businesses cannot afford to be technologically self-sufficient; large companies can. Much of the organized industrial research and development being carried out today is housed in large firms, especially in the chemical, electronic, aeronautical, and pharmaceutical industries. It is generally inaccessible to outsiders, however. In addition, these R&D efforts tend to be so concentrated as to limit their application to only a few sectors of the economy. Meanwhile, ancillary technologies go unused.

Well-defined and structured programs to facilitate technology transfer are urgently needed. Control Data's Technotec is one such program. It is a commercially available system in which massive amounts of information can be stored and quickly retrieved. Two types of information are included in the data base: descriptions of problems that need solving, and descriptions of technologies that may be applied to their solution. This arrangement enables providers and users of technology to meet in what amounts to a computerized marketplace. When a scientist or an inventor has an idea during the course of a university, government, or independent research project, he or she can list it with Technotec and advertise its availability to prospective buyers. Conversely, those who are seeking innovations can use the service to find out about technologies that may satisfy their needs. This interaction not only increases the chances that a particular idea will be used, but, more importantly, it makes innovation possible in response to a combination of market pull and technology push rather than technology push alone. Experience teaches that the most successful and least costly innovations are those which result from an early linkage between an idea and a need, because the further development of the idea can then be channeled to achieve a desired end.

Systems like Technotec provide one way of facilitating technology transfer; there are others. For example, the U.S. Department of Agriculture has a staff of extension service field agents in direct contact with farmers.

Agriculture takes technology transfer seriously and spends close to 50 percent of its annual R&D budget on it. Its program is large and very successful. In contrast, most other government agencies follow more traditional—and not as effective—methods of disseminating the results of their research and development, and spend as little as one percent or even less for that purpose. Industry has considerable difficulty in getting information from them. This is particularly true of agencies such as the Department of Defense, which rely principally on R&D documents as a means of transfer.

Funding for implementing a comprehensive approach to technology diffusion should be included in every government or government-sponsored research program. The funds should be used mainly to provide incentives—such as royalties—to individual researchers, thereby encouraging them to contribute their time and skills to the identification of commercial applications.

If government agencies can be characterized as inefficient when it comes to technology transfer, private industry may be more aptly described as reluctant. Vast amounts of under-utilized technology exist in industry. Most companies use only part of their stock in their own commercial activities; the remaining unused technologies may well have commercial applications elsewhere in the economy, and it is likely that technology utilized in one product could be applied to other products in the same or different industries. Yet these technologies are seldom shared due to a long-standing bottleneck: the concern for maintaining a proprietary position.

In the past, individual companies that assumed reasonable risk and expended sufficient technical effort to develop new products could expect an attractive return on investment. But circumstances are changing. Most of the easy things have already been done, and it is getting increasingly difficult to bring out new proprietary products—more expensive, more time-consuming, more risky. Industry has accordingly turned away from developing new products and focused on improving existing ones and cutting manufacturing costs. There have been a few significant breakthroughs in recent years, but the new technologies have been dispersed so rapidly that any initial business advantage has been lost. As a result, companies in most industries are currently producing and selling what amount to the same products; when they differ, it is usually with respect to design features that improve their appearance and/or user application.

Concern for a proprietary position in today's market is rooted more in habit than wisdom. While there are still good reasons to protect proprietary elements of the marketing process, this should no longer be a consideration in R&D. Instead, companies should be encouraged by means of incentives to make their technologies more readily available to one another. This would not only help to offset the growing costs of marketing technology, but also benefit society. The ability to benefit society should in itself be perceived as an incentive for effecting technology transfer. It seems only fair: all technology is, at least in part, a product of the educational system and, by extension, of the knowledge and technical efforts of others.

While the more efficient utilization of existing technologies would be to everyone's advantage, it would not be sufficient to solve society's major problems. For that, a whole new round of technological innovations will be needed. Special emphasis should be placed on technologies that will create new sources of energy and new materials.

Normally, the kind of technological development that is financed by private enterprise has a large enough payout and low enough risk that an acceptable return on investment in R&D is virtually assured. This is also the kind of development that results in products and services that meet conventional business tests rather than addressing society's fundamental needs. If diverse technologies were generated to meet social needs, these could in turn be potentially useful over a very broad range and could be applied quite profitably to the subsequent development of new products, processes, and services, as well as to improvements in existing ones. Because of the possible value to society of such projects, it is imperative for the government to join with private industry to pursue them.

More effective utilization of existing technology and expansion of R&D efforts cannot be achieved without far more cooperation than currently exists. Control Data has long recognized this fact, as shown by its basic strategy of addressing social needs as business opportunities in cooperation with other sectors of society.

Because society's problems are massive, massive resources are required to adequately address them—resources that are usually beyond individual companies and, in a number of instances, individual countries. Not even the United States can do everything on its own. International diffusion of technology is no less important than technology transfer on a national scale. While almost everyone is aware that exporting products contributes to the creation of new jobs within the domestic economy, relatively few people realize that, on balance, the export of technology—properly managed—could achieve the same results. This, by the way, should not be done on a cash basis, since the sale of technology does not directly create jobs, except for those relatively few personnel who are required to effect the transaction. In fact, the number of jobs resulting from this type of arrangement tends to decrease over time, depending on the extent to which products derived from exported technology are imported and displace American-made products.

Unless a technology has become obsolete, it is usually not in the best interests of a company or a country to simply sell it. Such a sale is virtually risk-free to the buyer, who not only acquires the technology itself, but also benefits from the prior investment of time and money that went into its development. Since the acquisition of technology can cut years off the time it takes to get a product to market, a cash sale can work to the seller's disadvantage.

The most economically desirable way to transfer technology is to exchange it—that is, to import and export technologies having equivalent values. This could be accomplished either by means of a direct exchange or indirectly through joint projects, jointly owned companies, or wholly owned subsidiaries. The latter option is becoming less acceptable to many countries who prefer to retain the controlling interest over businesses within their borders.

There is a growing, if still limited, awareness in the United States of the need for increased international cooperation. NASA is involved in a number of cooperative activities with other countries, and several joint research projects are now under way between the United States and the Soviet Union. One, the nuclear fusion project, was begun in 1974 and based on an innovative process developed by Soviet scientists. Another, the magneto-hydrodynamics research and development program (MHD), resulted in an initial savings to the United States of more than $150 million when it was decided that the two countries would jointly use a Soviet testing facility. Both sides are benefiting; the MHD program is progressing more quickly and with less risk of technical failure than it would be if either country was working independently. A third example of international cooperation is the United States-Israeli binational foundation for industrial research and development. Unfortunately, there are relatively few other examples to cite.

Something else that deserves consideration is the fact that there is virtually no technology exclusive to the United States. Department of Commerce statistics show that Europe and Japan today have essentially the same technologies we have; in addition, the rate with which they are generating industrial technology has begun to exceed ours in many areas. Studies by the National Science Board reveal that in the period between 1953 and 1958, some 80 percent of all major innovations originated in the United States. In 1959-1964, that figure fell to 67 percent, and between 1965 and 1973 it dropped to 57 percent.

One reason for this trend is the decline in R&D expenditures in the United States as a percentage of GNP at a time when other countries are providing financial incentives and allocating a much higher proportion of their resources to R&D. Of the top ten research organizations in the chemical industry, rated by the size of their R&D budgets, only three are American companies. Nuclear power plant technology is moving faster in Europe than in the United States, while Russia has surpassed us in both welding technology and titanium fabrication.

There are numerous areas in which the United States still

holds the lead, but by a margin of only a few years. For example, we are ahead in computer technology, but our lead is not overwhelming. European and Japanese computers are in many respects equivalent to American products, and competition from them is becoming stiff.

The most important conclusion to draw from these observations is that the United States does not have the resources to provide all of the technological innovations required to solve our major societal problems. We do have the best management and marketing resources in the world, however, and are thus ideally positioned to promote and benefit from technological cooperation with other countries.

The question has been raised as to whether it would be wise for the United States to assist in building up and strengthening the technological capabilities of other countries. In view of the fact that there is virtually no technology today that is exclusive to the United States, the answer seems clear: if we don't help those countries meet their technological needs, others will. And then we will lose in three ways. The value of our technology will decline; we will suffer from increased competition in the world markets; and we will not have access to other technologies that could give us a greater competitive edge in those markets.

Commercial considerations are not the only ones to keep in mind; there is also the matter of military implications. It is difficult to calculate the military risks involved in international technology transfers. Almost any commercial product, service, or technology, ranging from food and clothing to jet engines and electronic computers, can contribute to a country's military capability either directly or indirectly—in the latter case, by bolstering its economy. Since most military developments are covert, it is often hard to tell when a technology is being utilized specifically for military purposes. Thus, while the decision to exchange any particular item of technology should be based in part on its potential military benefit to the other country, the primary consideration should be that of what the United States will get in return.

There are, of course, elaborate government controls on the export of technologies with high military potential. It is uncertain whether they are very effective, however. Their imposition has done little to prevent the Soviet Union from building up its military power and meeting its major weapons objectives. On the other hand, the Department of Defense reports that Soviet progress in some important areas, such as electronics, has been slowed, thus making it possible for the United States to maintain weapons superiority longer in a number of key areas. Because we are really talking about tradeoffs—benefits and risks—and not embargoes, the results of levying such controls seem inconsistent at best.

For the past several years, we should have been asking ourselves whether the benefits we think we are getting from export controls—namely, lower military risks and reduced defense spending—are commensurate with our losses in the areas of jobs and business opportunities. While we have been holding back, foreign competitors have been selling equivalent or acceptable alternative products to the Soviet Union. Meanwhile, there has been nothing to stop the Soviets from developing their own products or leap-frogging the state of the art to a more advanced technology and posing an even greater military threat to us.

In numerous instances, NATO's coordinating committee on East-West trade, which approves export licenses, has denied them to domestic manufacturers in the United States. Over the past decade, Control Data alone has lost computer equipment business valued at $235 million; this represents an average of 1,100 American jobs per year sacrificed to foreign firms. Moreover, export controls have stimulated the Communist countries to develop their own computer industries. Today, virtually all of their needs for small- and medium-sized computers are being met internally. The only computer markets left for American companies are for larger computers and peripherals; these, too, will eventually shrink unless export restrictions are loosened.

Given even moderate relaxation of export controls, it is estimated that American sales of large computers and peripherals could build in ten years to an annual level representing 150,000 high-technology jobs. This is not a pie-in-the-sky figure. Similar increases have occurred in the past when export controls were eased. For example: from after World War II through most of the 1960s, the American government prohibited the export of Caterpillar earth-moving equipment to the U.S.S.R. and Eastern Europe. In the latter part of the 1960s, this prohibition was lifted. Immediately thereafter, sales of Caterpillar tractors and other products to those countries soared, creating thousands of jobs for Americans.

What is missing from our current export policy is a provision for the establishment of national priorities and guidelines for the development and application of technology. These should be described in terms of our most pressing social needs and opportunities. An analysis of possible benefits should also be provided, and it should include forecasts of the numbers and types of jobs that would be created or eliminated.

We should also begin keeping a national inventory of technology. Like most countries, we keep track of goods and services, but do not make a sufficient accounting of the value of technology transfers. Technology as a national resource is ultimately far more valuable than supplies of energy and food—items for which we go to great length and expense to compile records. We must maintain an accounting of technology trade balances not only because their volume is increasing, but also because this would serve to better inform the public of what is going on and increase their understanding of technology and its importance to society.

An aggressive promotion of worldwide technological cooperation should also be a significant part of our export policy. Finally, the policy should provide for an expanded and continuing education of the American public—including our politicians—of what technology is all about, how it meets basic societal needs, and how it affects employment.

I am convinced that such a policy would foster the export of virtually any industrial product or technology, given the appropriate conditions. The emphasis should be on expanding imports, not restricting them, with a single government agency being responsible for making the final decisions on specific items. Only those products or services embodying the most advanced technology would require the scrutiny of this agency; most technology transfers would occur under blanket agreements negotiated between governments. In those instances where military risk was a factor, the guiding principle should be the knowledge that a strong industrial base is the greatest asset to U.S. defense. Cases of particular concern could be reviewed by a high-level commission consisting of members with unbiased interests and broad perspectives.

There are many different ways to confront the issue of technological cooperation. Obviously, no simple approach will resolve the complex issues involved in both the domestic and international transfer of technology. If they are not resolved, however, our way of life—and our very survival—will be seriously endangered.

PART TWO

3

Education

The age of technology has brought higher standards of living to millions of people. Historically, the principal instrument of advancement has been education, which has provided students and workers with the skills and knowledge necessary to function in an increasingly complex industrial and commercial economy. But today there is mounting evidence that our educational system is no longer responding adequately to society's changing needs.

Underprivileged and disabled persons are being neglected. Gifted students are not being challenged. Many high schools are producing a steady stream of functional illiterates. We are faced on every side with the call to improve the quality and equality of education—and the ramifications of failing to do so go far beyond the walls of the classroom.

As a country, we are becoming less and less capable of coping with the rapidly accumulating supply of new information, and this in turn is impeding our productivity. We are no longer efficiently creating the kinds of products and services that could supply millions of desperate workers with jobs, and the training available for the jobs that do exist is woefully inadequate. Nor is the rest of the world

SOURCES

"Via Technology to a New Era in Education" address (published as part of a technology booklet series and also in the *Phi Delta Kappan Journal*), 1976 Congress and Exposition of the Society for Applied Learning Technology, Washington, D.C., July 22, 1976.

"Advanced Technology Is Bringing Major Improvements to Education" address, Annual Conference of the National Co-operative Education Association, Torquay (Torbay), England, U.K., April 4, 1980.

"Computer Technology, Cooperation and Engineering Education" address, American Society for Engineering Education, S.E. Regional Conference, Chattanooga, Tennessee, April 6, 1981.

"U.K. Education #2" address, United Kingdom, April 4, 1980.

"Education" address, Education Strategic Plan Meeting, Minneapolis, Minnesota, September 4, 1980.

any better off; an estimated three-quarters of a billion adults who live in developing countries can neither read nor write.

The problem stems primarily from the inexorable rise in the cost of traditional, labor-intensive education, which has taken one school system after another to the brink of bankruptcy. Efforts at reform have been sporadic, fragmented, and marked by duplication of effort. Teachers are continually re-inventing the wheel, and the prerogative of each to decide what is best for his or her students has resulted in only isolated applications of advanced technologies when it is precisely those technologies that could make the difference. Teachers are not solely to blame, however. College presidents, faculties, trustees, public school boards, and communities have insisted on maintaining the status quo despite clear indications that it is no longer working to anyone's advantage.

Fortunately, we have at hand the tools we need to revitalize our educational system. Developments in the field of electronics have furnished a base of advanced technologies that can be used to improve the quality, productivity, and availability of education. These are aptly illustrated by Control Data's system of computer-based education (CBE) called Personal Learning and Training Opportunity, or PLATO.

Control Data entered the CBE field in 1963, when we joined with the University of Illinois in an R&D program, financed in part by the National Science Foundation, that was designed to explore the feasibility of using computers in the teaching process. Our decision to engage in this venture was prompted by two factors. One was my own growing concern with the inadequacies of American education. The second can be traced back to the end of World War II, when I became interested in the commercial applications of the recently developed electronic digital computers.

At that time, analog computers were widely used to train Air Force and airline pilots by realistically simulating flight conditions. It seemed reasonable that substituting digital computers for analog computers could make such a training system much more flexible, since it could then be used for other types of training as well. In 1946, an investigation of this possibility showed that the costs would be prohibitive; electronic components were then quite expensive. By the early 1960s, far less costly components had been developed, and we were able to implement our earlier idea in cooperation with the University of Illinois.

In 1967, after government funding of approximately $22 million had been used to determine that CBE was indeed practicable, Control Data assumed major financial responsibility for what had by then become known as PLATO. All told, the company has spent more than $900 million to date on the development, refinement, and application of the PLATO system. We have continued to work with the University of Illinois, which is now one of more than 40 universities around the world engaged with Control Data in cooperative CBE projects.

Today PLATO is an educational delivery system of the first order. It employs virtually every type of media, including video and audio tapes and disks, slides, and digital inputs and outputs. It is extraordinarily versatile and has demonstrated its ability to provide accessible, affordable, and uniformly high-quality education and training.

A broad and flexible range of courses and lessons, called "courseware," is stored in a central computer or on flexible disks. The courseware is accessed through television-like terminals operated by users at their own pace. Materials are called up by means of a typewriter-like keyboard and a touch-sensitive screen and are displayed in the form of numbers, text, drawings, and animated graphics.

The system also includes a stand-alone version offered on the Control Data 110 microcomputer. The 110 is a standard CDC product which does not require a communication line to the central computer, but can, if desired, be linked to it.

PLATO responds to a student's needs in a way that is not possible in a typical classroom environment. It has infinite patience and an almost inexhaustible memory. It gives the student immediate feedback and encouragement while teaching, drilling, testing, grading, and diagnosing in an individualized, self-paced, easy-to-use manner. There is continuous interaction between the student and the

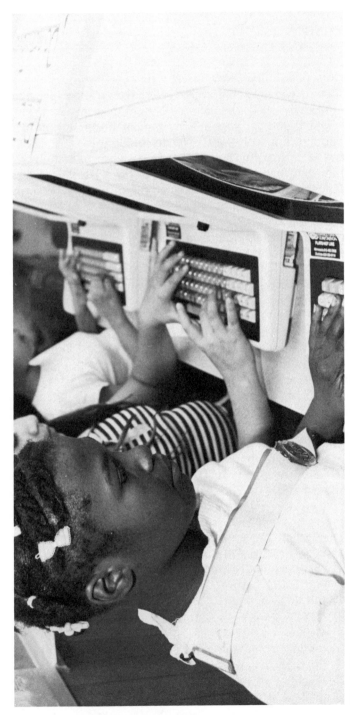

PLATO provides accessible, affordable, and uniformly high-quality education and training.

system, a give-and-take on a one-to-one basis.

PLATO can accommodate several users at the same time, regardless of the levels they are at or the subjects they are studying. The fast learner need not wait for the slow learner, and the slow learner is not embarrassed by having his or her rate of progress exposed to everyone else. In addition, PLATO has extensive record-keeping capabilities that free teachers from routine administrative tasks and allow them to concentrate on what they do best: giving students personal guidance and support.

Because it can update, flashback, review, explain, and simulate almost any activity, PLATO provides a unique learning experience for all types of individuals, including small children; grade school, high school, and college students; blue- and white-collar workers; supervisors; and professional and management personnel. Courseware titles range from astronomy to zoology. Lessons are generated by several hundred experts who are constantly adding to the more than 10,000 hours already housed in the company's library. Some 250 authors are under direct contract with Control Data, while several others work on a royalty basis.

When PLATO was first introduced into the marketplace in the mid-1970s, the three major deterrents to its use were cost, the lack of sufficient courseware, and resistance on the part of the educational establishment. Since that time, the first two have largely been obviated. The diminishing cost of electronic components has driven the price down and continues to do so. In the past three years, for example, the total cost for the average subscriber has been halved, and it is anticipated that service charges will be halved again over the next five years. In contrast, conventional labor-intensive education and training costs are expected to rise by more than 50 percent. As far as courseware is concerned, the amount of lesson materials grows substantially with each passing year as more leading educators join the ranks of PLATO authors.

The third deterrent to PLATO's widespread use has not yet been overcome, however. The educational establishment is still reluctant to welcome the computer into the teaching process. This is frustrating, but not all that surprising when one considers that 200 years went by after the book came into being before it was commonly used by teachers. What has happened is that PLATO has been forced to prove itself first outside the realm of public education.

Control Data's strategy has been to enter a few chosen fields where resistance is relatively low and increase its commitment of resources gradually. Thus far, we have focused on education and training for business and industry; proprietary vocational education; education and training for the disadvantaged and the disabled; continuing education; and education and training for developing countries.

Business and industry have generally been more receptive to CBE than other sectors of society. This is largely due to the shift in industry from manufacturing to services, which, when combined with declining rates of labor productivity, has accentuated the importance of employee training. Companies under pressure to compete and show profits are finding it necessary to devote larger outlays to training and retraining their workers. This is especially true for small businesses, where narrow margins for error make it essential to have well-trained employees to offset the economies of scale enjoyed by larger competitors. Because traditional training methods for industry employees are very expensive, many companies have been attracted to PLATO and what it has to offer.

Businesses can obtain PLATO in a variety of ways. For example, they can lease or purchase Control Data 110 terminals, which are then installed on their premises and connected, if desired, with Control Data's central PLATO computer via cable, satellite, or telephone. This subscription service has two distinct advantages for small companies whose training requirements are ongoing and expensive: a low entry cost, and a minimal commitment of capital and resources. Large companies may opt to purchase PLATO computer and terminal facilities.

Currently, a number of public utilities either own or lease PLATO terminals and are using them to train power-plant personnel in several complex and sometimes critical areas. Pharmaceutical companies find PLATO invaluable for helping their first-line plant supervisors to maintain quality control and ensuring that sales representatives are thoroughly familiar with new products. The National Association of Security Dealers has contracted with Control Data to train its registered account executives and has benefited greatly from having PLATO administer its certification examinations. Because the computer can select questions randomly, an almost infinite variety of tests is possible, and trainee strengths and weaknesses can be audited on a continual basis.

Those companies which neither subscribe to PLATO nor purchase it may have access to the system through the Control Data learning centers located in more than 100 cities throughout the United States and western Europe. Each center is equipped with a PLATO system and staffed by experienced personnel. The centers are ideal for individuals who wish to take specific courses or broaden their expertise in certain areas, and for organizations with short-term training needs and large numbers of geographically dispersed employees. The American Chemical Society, the Institute of Electrical and Electronic Engineers in the United States, and the American Management Association are only a few of the professional organizations that have used Control Data learning centers.

In the field of proprietary vocational education, the largest users of PLATO other than the learning centers are the Control Data Institutes (CDIs). CDIs are vocational schools that specialize in the teaching of computer programming, operation, and maintenance, along with data entry and word processing. Currently, CDIs are found in 40 cities, 13 of them outside the United States in countries such as England, France, Germany, Canada, and Australia.

The first CDI was established in 1963, long before PLATO became operational, in response to Control Data's pressing need for qualified computer technicians. Until then, the only ones we could find—individuals who had received their training in the military or in vocational schools—were not adequately prepared, even though most of them had spent at least two years studying to become technicians. After we hired them, we were forced to provide them with several additional months of training at our expense. Control Data Institutes were founded on the premise that nine months are sufficient to prepare someone for an entry-level technician's position, provided that the courses are well-designed, well-focused, and well-taught.

The distinguishing features of the CDIs, especially since they began using PLATO, have been high-quality training and an excellent placement record. In 1978, the American Society of Training and Development gave the Control Data Institutes its prestigious award for service and excellence—the only one given that year. Of the approximately 60,000 individuals who have been graduated from the institutes since their inception, nearly 95 percent of those who sought placement assistance have been hired by computer manufacturers and users in all types of businesses, as well as industry, government, research, and education. A growing number of students are college graduates who combine their technical training with undergraduate degrees. Many CDI graduates go back for advanced technical courses or broaden their career possibilities with the study of management and financial subjects.

A third important market for PLATO is education and training for the disadvantaged. In cooperation with leading educators, Control Data has developed two programs over the past several years that have proved especially significant: the Basic Skills learning system, and the General Education learning system.

The Basic Skills curriculum is designed to help underachieving students advance from a third-grade to an eighth-grade equivalency in reading, language, and math skills. The learning system has been taken into tough environments—the inner city, poverty-stricken rural areas, prison systems—and the results have been very impressive. In Baltimore, 24 functionally illiterate adults advanced almost one full grade level in reading after only 22 hours of instruction, 20 of them on PLATO. Another group of 200 Florida students advanced an average of one grade level after spending 14 hours on PLATO. It takes about 150 hours of traditional instruction, not counting homework, before students of average motivation and ability can make similar progress.

The General Education learning system is a high school curriculum consisting of lessons corresponding to the five sections of the General Education Development (GED) examination: reading, mathematics, writing, science, and social studies. It also offers courses describing the GED exam and how to take it. This program meets the needs of high school students who require remedial assistance; of advanced students who want to learn faster and pursue a richer curriculum; and of the thousands of dropouts who cannot get or hold jobs without first acquiring a GED certificate.

Disabled persons can also lead more productive lives through PLATO. Virtually all of the machines and instruments used by disabled individuals to provide them with varying degrees of physical capabilities can be adapted to PLATO; similarly, PLATO can be modified in a number of ways to make it more accessible. The keyboard can be changed to allow paraplegics to operate it with a mouth-stick. Another modification makes it possible for those with severe cerebral palsy to use the terminal. Still another, called a Teletractor, is under development for the deaf. It will incorporate a waistbelt that translates sounds into skin sensations; when an audio device sounds a word or sentence, an electronic device attached to the waistbelt will convert the frequencies into rippling sensations on the wearer's stomach, and the word or sentence will simultaneously be flashed onto the screen of the PLATO terminal.

For the severely disabled population, a program called Homework offers training and employment alternatives. Participants can learn to be computer programmers or to perform other occupations on PLATO terminals installed in their homes. They are then placed in jobs they can do at home. Homework has evolved into a computer network of disabled individuals learning different skills at different rates while sharing the learning experience.

There is an increasing demand for continuing education,

and Control Data is responding by making PLATO courses available at its own learning centers and a number of educational institutions. The courses cover a broad range of subjects—biology, chemistry, physics, engineering, mathematics, the social sciences, music, and several languages including English, French, Spanish, Greek, Russian, Latin, and basic Chinese. Computer-based continuing education has particular appeal for working persons who have completed their initial education, do not have time to attend courses at universities or community colleges, and want to pursue their studies further at times and places convenient to them with materials that meet their needs.

Most recently, PLATO has been used for education and training in developing countries. Two settings have been chosen for entry into this area: South Africa and Jamaica. Although the two countries are very different—in South Africa, for example, developing country conditions exist side-by-side with those of a developed country— PLATO's versatility makes it ideally suited for both.

Control Data Corporation has been doing business in South Africa for many years, and we have learned firsthand about that country's problems, most of which center around apartheid. While we strongly abhor apartheid, we simultaneously recognize the crying need of South Africa's black people for better education and training. Refusing to deal with South Africa because of its segregationist policies will not make that need go away. The black population is growing by an average of four percent annually, and traditional educational methods simply cannot keep up. The answer lies in advanced technology, primarily CBE.

South Africa has a serious teacher shortage. In South African terminology, it is estimated that 25,000 white teachers, 22,000 coloured teachers, and 250,000 black teachers will be needed by 1990; the actual numbers of teachers available at that time will fall far short of the mark unless teacher training is greatly improved. PLATO can serve an important function by preparing future teachers and upgrading the skills of existing teachers, who can in turn use their training to instruct others.

At this stage, PLATO is used in South Africa mainly for industrial education and training. In 1979, a PLATO learning center opened at the Control Data Institute in downtown Johannesburg for the purpose of training and placing black computer programmers. Since June of that year, 197 students have attended the Institute, and a 100 percent placement rate has been achieved for all students who sought placement. Fifty-five of those were non-whites.

The University of the Western Cape is using PLATO for remedial education to reduce the dropout rate. And, as part of a long-range strategy, a substantial amount of effort is being devoted to the development of courseware specifically aimed at meeting the unique needs of South Africa's black population.

In Jamaica, PLATO is expected to perform a vital role in Jamaican Opportunity for Business Success (JOBS), a for-profit consortium whose participants include Control Data and other U.S. companies; the U.S. government; Jamaican companies; and the government of Jamaica.

The unemployment rate in Jamaica is currently around 30 percent, and there are some 350,000 young people between the ages of 15 and 21 who are functionally illiterate. Thus, the program will focus initially on teacher training, the teaching of basic skills, and high school equivalency and vocational education. Technical training courses for specific occupations will also be available. JOBS will contract with the Jamaican government to furnish these services through PLATO, and small companies will be established to develop CBE courseware both for use in Jamaica and for export to other countries.

Since its entry into the marketplace in the 1970s, PLATO has been shown to be an extremely versatile and effective teaching tool. The possibilities of the system seem virtually limitless. Nevertheless, the public school system—where PLATO might be expected to reach the most students—has continued to balk at CBE in general. There have been some notable exceptions, including a number of primary and secondary school systems and the universities of Delaware, Colorado, Quebec, California

State, and Florida State, but public education as a whole has yet to accept computers into their curricula.

A number of reasons might be cited for this continued resistance. One is the reluctance to change on the part of many teachers and administrators. Another is the lack of incentive educational institutions have to improve their productivity. Most schools do not have to compete for students, and their funding is usually based on the number of students who attend rather than the number who complete their education—a system that essentially encourages schools to keep students around longer than necessary.

Some educators are opposed to CBE because they feel that technology takes away the human touch that is so important to teaching. On the contrary, computers can bring a human dimension to learning that many schools fail to impart. Those who doubt this should see the highly visible satisfaction that disadvantaged young students get from their initial experience with a PLATO terminal. For the first time in their lives, they have a world of knowledge at their fingertips; for the first time in their lives, they are in control.

The main reason why educators are unwilling to embrace CBE is the fear that it will lead to fewer jobs for teachers. This perceived threat is true to an extent; the widespread use of the computer would herald a period of readjustment for the teaching profession. Other professions have faced similar challenges, however, and have not only survived, but benefited from them. For example, the introduction of the computer resulted at first in decreasing employment for engineers. Along the way, it was discovered that the computer could free engineers from many repetitive and boring tasks and allow them to be more creative. There are more engineers today than ever before.

Similarly, the implementation of CBE might initially cut down on the numbers of jobs available for teachers. At the same time, it would enrich the task of teaching and enhance its professional status. Fewer hours would be spent on imparting information, and more could be devoted to working with individual students. The growing emphasis on continuing education would open up new teaching positions with a consequent increase in total employment. Finally, educators would be needed to design courseware. In any event, change would take place slowly, and it would be possible for teachers to accommodate themselves to it without undue hardship.

Many educational administrators resist CBE in its present form because they believe that very powerful, low-cost microcomputers will eventually be found in every classroom and home. They do not want to make a large capital investment today for fear that it would preclude them from implementing the superior technologies that are sure to come tomorrow. What these educators fail to understand is that CBE—specifically PLATO—consists of far more than hardware. Although certain microcomputers are improving with respect to performance, their capabilities still fall far short of PLATO's. And compared to Control Data's extensive courseware holdings, the supporting library of microcomputer instructional materials now available is sketchy and inadequate. The real long-term benefits of CBE will be derived when the focus shifts from hardware to applications and courseware; Control Data's PLATO strategy for the 1980s anticipates this shift. Rather than waiting for the unproved technology of the future, educators should commit themselves to using the tools that are available in the present.

Society can no longer be served by traditional educational methods; they are simply too costly and too limited. Ultimately, the computer and the score of CBE activities generated in its wake will have the capacity to reach every individual in the world and provide better access to knowledge that will both enrich their personal lives and give them more control over their destinies. The stage has been set; the scenario is no idle dream.

4

Employment

Unemployment and underemployment are the most pressing of the myriad social and economic problems with which we are faced today. Reports show that the number of unemployed workers as a proportion of the total labor force in the United States has varied between 3.5 percent, or 2.8 million, in 1969 and 9.0 percent, or 9.9 million, in early 1982. The published statistics do not reveal the true dimensions of the problem, however. Because of the way they are compiled, they omit large groups of unemployed individuals, including those who are willing to work, but have given up looking for jobs; those who are partially disabled; and others who are unable to take on full-time employment for whatever reason.

The statistics also fail to indicate how the impact of structural unemployment—the result of an imbalance between the structure of the economy and the occupational structure of the labor force—has led to decreasing job opportunities for unskilled, illiterate, and older workers, as well as for skilled workers who cannot find jobs in their

SOURCES

"Technology and Full Employment" address (also published as part of a technology booklet series), Minnesota Full Employment Action Council, Minneapolis, Minnesota, September 6, 1977. (Placed in *Congressional Record* by Senator Hubert H. Humphrey, October 28, 1977.)

"Technology and the Handicapped" address (also published as part of a technology booklet series), Annual Awards Program at Camp Courage, Golden Valley, Minnesota, May 16, 1979.

Statement by W.C. Norris to the House of Representatives, Committee on the Budget, Task Force on Inflation, and Subcommittee on Science, Research and Technology, Joint Hearings on Measures To Reduce Inflation, Washington, D.C., July 23, 1979.

"Technology and Unemployment" address, National Alliance of Business, Minneapolis, Minnesota, September 19, 1979.

"Technology and Disadvantaged Youth" address, National Association of Counties Convention, San Antonio, Texas, November 25, 1980.

"A Million Jobs for Disadvantaged Youths" essay, October 1980.

own areas and are not able to move elsewhere. Nor do they reveal how much underemployment is due to the fact that the average educational requirement for nearly half of all the jobs in the United States is only 10.5 years. Many people are over-qualified and over-prepared in terms of their education for the jobs that do exist.

Finally, no quantitative data can begin to measure the human and social costs of broken families, low self-esteem, futility, anger, and the higher mortality, illness, and crime rates that go hand-in-hand with unemployment. Nor are there figures to represent the billions of dollars in potential production that have been lost forever.

Achieving adequate employment should be our number one priority, but we have not yet demonstrated the willingness to commit the resources needed to meet the challenge. Not enough requisite planning is being done on the national, state, or local levels—or, for that matter, within the private sector. Witness, for example, the reluctance on the part of Congress to pass legislation realistically designed to bring about full employment. Witness also our failure to provide jobs and adequate training for the structurally unemployed and the disadvantaged, particularly the young, whose rates of unemployment have for many years ranged between 30 and 50 percent.

The requirements for effecting long-term solutions to these problems are reasonably clear. To prevent unemployment from becoming even more critical over the next decade, we must create close to 20 million new jobs. To increase the overall productivity of the labor force, we must emphasize the creation of skilled jobs. To reduce both structural unemployment and underemployment, we must upgrade the training and skills of workers. The only way to achieve these goals is through a comprehensive full employment program.

The leadership for such a program must be assumed by business acting in cooperation with other major sectors of society. The program must do three things: generate new jobs, get people job-ready, and take jobs to people. Only business has the resources necessary to manage a program of this extent; only business can trigger the technological innovations needed to stimulate economic growth, found new industries, and provide millions of private-sector jobs. Both large and small business must take the initiative in improving worker training and taking jobs to the structurally unemployed and immobile members of the labor force.

The feasibility of taking jobs to people has been clearly demonstrated by Control Data's experience with putting manufacturing facilities in economically depressed urban and rural areas. Our experience had its beginnings when we located a plant in a poverty-stricken section of north Minneapolis, the scene of riots and fires during the summer of 1967.

The doors of the Northside plant opened in January of 1968 to a chorus of forecasts that it would never work. Critics predicted that the plant would be vandalized and its work force would fail to become efficient. They were wrong. By 1970, three more plants had been established in poverty areas: one in St. Paul, Minnesota; one in Washington, D.C.; and one in a depleted coal mining area in eastern Kentucky. In 1980 and 1981, two more were opened in San Antonio, Texas, and Bemidji, Minnesota. Together the six plants now employ nearly 2,000 people.

Control Data's decision to locate a plant in an economically disadvantaged community in Minneapolis stemmed from two parallel motivations: the need for added capacity to meet the growing demand for our products, and the belief that business has certain societal responsibilities. Realizing that we had to open a new plant somewhere, and recognizing the urgent need for employment among impoverished urban residents, we concluded that both objectives might be met simultaneously.

We were influenced by yet another factor. Since its inception, Control Data had been committed to equal employment opportunity, but we were dissatisfied with what we had accomplished so far. We had tried to attract minorities to our suburban plants, but we had not been able to make substantial progress toward that goal. Thus, locating a plant in a minority community seemed a reasonable thing to do. We have since learned that the success of that plant has served to establish our credibility in the minority community and has strengthened our entire corporate-wide equal opportunity effort.

We located a plant in a poverty-stricken section of north Minneapolis, the scene of riots and fires during the summer of 1967.

During the early years of its growth, Control Data had opened several new plants, most of them in small rural towns throughout the Upper Midwest. We knew that people who were totally unfamiliar with electronics could be trained and developed into productive workers. In the case of the Northside plant, we had to adapt this process to the radically different environment of the inner city. To that end, we were careful to follow a set of simple but essential guiding principles that were to bear heavily on the success of our Northside installation and later inner-city plants.

First, we viewed the establishment of the plant as a business venture that was expected to return an attractive profit over the long term—not as a philanthropic act.

Second, we considered start-up costs in the same way we consider research and development expenditures for a new product—as strategic outlays vital to our future growth.

Third, we made our commitment to the project widely visible both inside and outside the company. The plant we built was new, equipped with the most advanced facilities, and supervised by top management personnel. In addition, it was given responsibility for an important product line, thus making Control Data as dependent on its success as the people who worked there.

Fourth, we paid special attention to the needs of the employee population. Traditional skills-training programs and written instructions posted in the plant were modified to accommodate persons with lower reading levels. Wages and benefits were competitive with rates in the area. Trainers and trainees alike were given time to learn their tasks adequately and to understand the rights and responsibilities of both the employees and the company.

Finally, we adopted the policy of solving unusual problems promptly rather than kicking them around. "Whatever it takes" became the motto that drove our initial efforts at Northside, as well as those of our later inner-city plants.

We had help. Government funding was made available to train potential employees in basic skills. We solicited the advice and counsel of community leaders, and they in turn provided us with valuable insights about the neighborhood and its problems and suggested possible solutions. The link that was forged between the community and the company in those early days has remained strong over the years.

What does it take to make a project like Northside work? Sometimes it takes a lot. When the plant began operating, there were no child-care facilities in the vicinity. Since many of the employees were female heads of households with young children, it was obvious that child care would have to be provided if we were going to meet our goal of employing and retaining people who lived in the area. We again enlisted the support of the community and, in 1971, helped to start the Northside Child Development Center in a vacant 80-year-old school building. Five years later, the center was moved into a new building specifically designed for that purpose. Ninety percent of the funds for construction came from private donations and loans from local firms.

Today the Northside Child Development Center cares for approximately 140 children ranging in age from six weeks to 13 years. A staff of trained personnel conducts a carefully designed program that emphasizes personal, social, and physical development, arts and crafts, the sciences, and black history and awareness. The center is a non-profit corporation controlled by a board of parents, business people, and community leaders. Operating expenses are met by fees and donations from parents, local tax revenues, and contributions from several Minneapolis businesses.

Northside presented Control Data with problems other than child care, some of which did not at first have clear solutions. For example, many of its employees were unable to obtain credit. We responded by making loans available to them through our Commercial Credit subsidiary. Occasionally, employees experienced legal problems—some spent time in jail—which caused them to be absent from work and hampered the productivity of their work group. When necessary, one of our lawyers would go to the local jail with bail bonds and get people back on the job. More importantly, we offered counseling and ongoing legal assistance to those employees who needed it until their problems were resolved.

Still another problem centered on our standard employment form, which requires employees to list their prior work experience, educational background, and references, and to note any prior arrests and convictions. Many Northside employees had no work experience, no need for a full page on which to record their educational history, and no useful references, and some had been arrested more times than there was room for on the form. We developed a new form that asked for only two pieces of information: the employee's name, and the name of someone who could be reached in an emergency. In essence, we made it known that we were far more interested in the person's future than in his or her past.

It cost $2.5 million to bring the Northside plant up to the efficiency level of our suburban plants; $1.5 million from the government, and $1 million from Control Data. Considering that we now have a smoothly functioning production operation, that most employees stay on for an average of more than six years, and that we have been able to apply what we learned from Northside to the establishment of five additional plants in other poverty-stricken areas, the payoff has been a handsome one—comparable to what we might have achieved with a similar investment in product R&D.

Although the Northside plant and the Child Development Center made it possible for many area residents to find employment, we discovered that there were other job seekers who were unable to work during normal eight-hour shifts. These included female heads of households with school-age children, and high school, vocational school, and college students who needed money either to stay in school or to supplement their families' incomes. To address this problem, we decided early in 1970 to open a plant that would employ part-time workers exclusively. The site chosen was a renovated bowling alley in the economically distressed Selby area of St. Paul, Minnesota.

While the Selby plant is not responsible for a standardized product line, it performs the important function of assembling and distributing thousands of software and hardware manuals to Control Data customers around the world. It also handles various types of corporate mailings such as annual reports, employee publications, and the like. Previously, these services were purchased from outside vendors at nearly twice the cost.

In 1973, Selby began generating outside revenue by selling its services to businesses and government agencies, and in 1974 a new 15,000-square-foot facility was opened to accommodate the growth of the operation. Built principally by minority contractors, this was the first new industrial facility to be constructed in that part of the Selby area since 1889. The project has served as a catalyst within the neighborhood: other new businesses have opened, houses are being renovated, and a substantial number of new houses are under construction.

Currently, the Selby plant's work force numbers over 330. The first of three shifts is staffed primarily by mothers of school-age children, and the other two are staffed by students. Using part-time employees in a conventional work environment has proved to be a sound idea, especially for jobs that require unremitting concentration. It has resulted in an additional bonus: more than 150 Selby employees have since left their part-time jobs for more skilled and better-paying full-time employment at other Control Data facilities and Minneapolis-St. Paul companies.

Both the Northside and Selby plants have shown that jobs can be taken to people and that people can be trained to do them. They demonstrate the need for a massive training program aimed at upgrading the skills and productivity of our nation's labor force. It should be noted that there are already several existing programs, both in government and the private sector, which have helped workers to make a rapid, permanent transition into full-time private employment. One is the long-established apprenticeship program, sponsored by the government but supported mainly by employers and unions, that trains more than 250,000 apprentices each year. Both the National Alliance of Business and an organization known as Chicago United help and encourage small and large companies to employ minority workers. A number of companies, including Chase Manhattan Bank, Equitable Life Assurance, and the Continental Illinois Bank and Trust Company, also provide special training courses for their employees. In addition, the federally funded Skill Training and Improvement Program (STIP), launched in 1977, has successfully coordinated jobs and training for thousands of people.

But these and other programs, while admirable, fall far short of what is required, especially where the disadvantaged are concerned. Various public policies aimed at providing assistance for the disadvantaged often lack clearly stated objectives and end up being fragmented, spasmodic, and poorly coordinated. The degree to which they involve business is minuscule compared with what is needed and what business is capable of doing. For example, in 1979, the Opinion Research Corporation conducted a survey of 800 business executives to determine their reaction to the government's $400 million Employment Opportunities Pilot Program (EOP), which trains the hard-to-employ for jobs in private business and industry. In spite of the fact that both the National Alliance of Business and the Labor Department had spent months laying the groundwork for the program, only 12 percent of those interviewed had heard about it. After the program was explained to them, only 15 percent said that their companies would be "very likely" to provide jobs, and 39 percent said "somewhat likely."

This response is indicative of a widespread indifference to the problem. There is an acute need to educate and train youths living in high-poverty areas where unemployment rates have remained at unacceptable levels for over a decade, and this need is not being met. Most programs designed to address the issue of unemployment are not very effective, and the thousands of community-based organizations that are dedicated to helping lack the necessary resources. It is high time for business to take the initiative by formulating and implementing a comprehensive program.

A key element in such a program would be high-quality, readily accessible, and affordable education and training. Given the nationwide use of computer-based education and a span of three years, it would be possible for a million disadvantaged youths to learn basic skills, achieve high school equivalency, and receive vocational training. By the end of the third year, the stream of functionally illiterate disadvantaged youths pouring out of our nation's high schools could be cut off.

But disadvantaged youths need more than training alone. The program would also have to provide counseling and help in removing barriers to employment caused by personal problems; part-time jobs during the training period; and instruction in job-seeking skills. As an incentive, it would also have to assure participants that full-time jobs would be waiting for them at the completion of the training cycle.

To many, this type of program might sound too involved and extensive to be practicable. Control Data believes otherwise. We already have a program like the one just described, and it is working.

Our Fair Break program prepares disadvantaged young persons to find and keep jobs, and makes jobs available to them. More than 50 Fair Break programs are now operating around the country and delivering innovative training in basic skills, job readiness, life management, and job-seeking skills. Students spend an average of four months in the program while working part-time; the part-time employment allows them both to generate income and to discover and identify problems they may need to resolve before seeking permanent employment. More than 5,000 students have completed Fair Break programs since the first one began in May of 1978. On the average, 87 percent have advanced either to further training or jobs, and 72 percent of those placed have stayed on the job for six months or longer.

Most of the part-time jobs provided during Fair Break training are supplied by big business, primarily because it has the staff resources needed to give disadvantaged youths the extra attention they require. In contrast, small business accounts for a larger percentage of the full-time positions participants go into following the preparation process. The variety and flexibility inherent in small businesses make it possible for them to employ disadvantaged youths who would have difficulty accommodating themselves to the more standard employment patterns of larger companies.

The Fair Break program is funded primarily by CETA. Input on program direction and courseware development is supplied by the Fair Break Advisory Council, which consists of local CETA agency officials, educators, and representatives from community-based organizations. Incidentally, this is one of the first times that business has asked representatives of the public sector to serve in an advisory capacity, and their participation has improved the program significantly.

The experience gained from Fair Break has resulted in two other programs aimed at meeting the needs of disadvantaged youth: Advanced Career Employment and Training (ACET) and Career Outreach.

ACET began in 1979 when Control Data received a unique $3.3 million contract from the Department of Labor to prepare some 300 Job Corps youths from all over the country for jobs in the computer industry. One hundred students were trained as computer technicians and subsequently employed by Control Data. One hundred more were trained for non-technical entry-level jobs, and those who completed the program were again provided with jobs within Control Data. An additional 100 were assisted in finding entry-level positions with other companies in the Minneapolis-St. Paul area.

The contract was completed in February of 1982. The success of the technician training portion of the ACET program is particularly impressive: of the 113 Job Corps youths recruited, 96 finished an intensive nine-month training program and were placed in jobs at annual salaries of approximately $14,000.

Career Outreach helps disadvantaged youths to get started in careers by linking education and work experience. It began in September 1981 in Minneapolis, St. Paul, and Toledo. Initially, ten students were selected in Minneapolis and ten more in St. Paul; these numbers were expanded to 20 in each city. In Toledo, the program is somewhat broader and involves more students.

Career Outreach combines the resources of high schools, universities, and businesses to offer participants a unique opportunity to shape their futures. Students chosen for the program begin working in grades 10 or 11, part-time during the school year and full-time in summer. Their eligibility is certified by a unit of city or county government. During high school, counseling similar to that offered through Fair Break is made available to help students overcome barriers to employment. After high school, participants continue on to vocational training or college, financed in part by loans and in part by job income.

Fair Break, ACET, and Career Outreach are examples of the types of programs that are urgently needed and should be replicated nationwide. Implementing them is expensive, however. Unless business can expect to recover the costs they incur in training students, giving them part-time jobs, and placing them in full-time jobs when their training is completed, it is doubtful that they will get involved to any great extent. Thus, government must be willing to provide them with tax incentives.

Rather than representing a net loss to the government, such tax credits would in fact be a good investment. Studies have shown that, on the average, a job is worth some $53,000 per year to the federal government. If 25 percent of that $53,000 value were shared with employers of disadvantaged youths in the form of tax credits extending over a ten-year period, all parties would benefit handsomely. Employers would acquire experienced employees; students would be launched on careers; and society as a whole would realize a net gain.

Rising unemployment is a problem of such magnitude that we can no longer afford to ignore it or hope that it will simply go away; the statistics clearly demonstrate that it will not. Business must take the initiative in planning comprehensive employment and training programs and putting them into operation. We have within our grasp the resources we need to affect the lives of millions of people and change them for the better, and we must start recognizing our obligation to do so.

5

Small Business

Small business has always been an integral and vital part of American life. Prior to the onset of rapid industrialization, it dominated the economy. Following the emergence of large corporations in the late nineteenth century, observers predicted that small companies would become obsolete with the eventual nationalization of the economy; despite major changes in the social, economic, and political environment, however, small businesses in America have persisted in significant numbers. They constitute approximately 99.8 percent of the companies in the United States, produce about 38 percent of the nation's goods and services, and account for more than 47 percent of the jobs in the private sector.

A widespread preoccupation with industrial and commercial giants has obscured the contributions small business has made to America's growth and development. For example, few people are aware that between 1953 and 1973 close to half of the major innovations introduced into U.S. industry came from firms with fewer than 1,000 employees—and a quarter of those originated in firms with fewer than 100. In addition, small business has outshone big business with respect to job-creating efficiency. As a

SOURCES

"Rebirth of Technological Innovation via Small Business" address (also published as part of a technology booklet series), American Physical Society, Chicago, Illinois, March 23, 1979.

"Small Business: A Great Resource for a Country, A Great Opportunity for Big Business" address, American Club of Stockholm, Stockholm, Sweden, February 6, 1980.

Testimony by W.C. Norris before the Senate Select Committee on Small Business, Hearings on Economic Growth, Washington, D.C., July 1, 1980.

"Big Business Helps Small Business To Improve Productivity and Create Jobs" essay, June 24, 1980.

"Technology for Community Enterprise Development" address, Second National Conference on New Enterprise Development, Washington, D.C., March 2, 1981.

1979 MIT study demonstrated, small companies were responsible for 7.4 million, or 78 percent, of the 9.6 million new jobs added to the U.S. economy between 1969 and 1976.

Today small business continues to serve as a symbol of opportunity and enterprise in our system of values, but there is reason to be concerned about its future. The cumulative impact of government regulations, the escalating cost and concomitant scarcity of capital, the decreasing availability of technology, and heightened competition from big business have combined over the past decade to bring about a serious deterioration in the climate for small business. The mortality rate of new companies is shocking: only about 20 percent of those that are started each year manage to survive, and close to 400,000 fail annually. These figures affect not only would-be entrepreneurs, but also the millions of Americans who could be sharing in the abundant benefits and countless skilled jobs that would have resulted had these businesses been successful.

If we are to save small business, we—meaning big business, government, non-profit and for-profit endeavors, community organizations, and all other major segments of our society—must join in a massive and systematic effort to nurture the innovative potential and profitable growth of existing small businesses and stimulate the creation of still more new businesses and small firms. We already have at hand the technological, professional, and management resources needed to implement this systematic effort. However, many of these lie dormant or underutilized in corporations, government offices, universities, and other places. We must find ways to assemble them, apply them, and make them more accessible to small business. To achieve these objectives, we must revise existing government policies and commercial practices that inhibit the use of these resources, find better ways of distributing them, and enlist the aid of community-based organizations in coordinating and focusing the talents of business, academia, and state and local governments.

In 1978, I chaired a committee which made a number of

recommendations to Jordan Baruch, then Assistant Secretary of Commerce, aimed at making capital and management resources more available to small, technically oriented enterprises. Specifically, the committee advocated the following: (1) reducing capital gains taxes to 25 percent for firms employing between 100 and 500 workers, and to 10 percent for firms with fewer than 100 employees; (2) deferring the capital gains tax for firms that re-invest the proceeds from their stock sales in small businesses; (3) raising to $200,000 the threshold at which the full corporate income tax takes effect for small businesses; (4) increasing the carry-forward provisions for small business start-up losses from five to ten years; and (5) restoring qualified stock option plans for key employees.

In 1977-78, the 95th Congress reduced the maximum tax on capital gains to 28 percent; in 1979-80, the 96th Congress followed this example by reducing it further to 20 percent. Pending legislation reflects two more of the committee's recommendations: a carry-forward period of ten years for start-up losses, and the deferral of taxes when the proceeds from stock sales are re-invested in small business.

The committee also suggested means by which research could be further stimulated and the technology developed by big business and government be made more useful to small enterprises. These included: (1) requiring each government agency to allocate at least 10 percent of its R&D budget to helping small business; (2) allowing small companies to establish and maintain tax-deductible reserves for R&D use in times of financial hardship; and (3) redirecting some government-sponsored research into improving small farms and food processors, and making food production less capital- and fossil fuel-intensive.

The first two of these recommendations are contained in pending legislation, but little attention has been given to date to the redirection of funds for agricultural purposes. There are two exceptions: the National Science Foundation recently set aside some funds for research applicable to small-scale agriculture, and the Department of Agriculture has stated its intention to do likewise. Generally speaking, though, no major legislative action has been taken on these matters. This may be due to a lack of awareness of the tremendous potential inherent in small-scale agriculture and food processing. Control Data is one of the few companies to recognize this potential and act on it; since 1979, we have been committed through Rural Ventures to fostering the development of small-scale agriculture and food-processing enterprises.

Finally, the committee made two recommendations designed to improve the diffusion of technology to small businesses: (1) that each government agency allocate five percent of its R&D funds for technology transfer; and (2) that tax incentives be provided to induce large companies to make their technologies more available to small companies.

Traditional methods of technology transfer have proved ineffective. Were government agencies to begin devoting five percent of their R&D budgets to technology transfer, these funds could be used primarily to encourage individual researchers to contribute their time and skills to identifying commercial applications. The incentives could be tied to the benefits realized from the transfers of the technologies involved.

On October 21, 1980, Congress acknowledged the feasibility of this idea by passing the Stevenson-Wydler Technology Innovation Act of 1980, which mandates that each government agency allot one-half of one percent of its R&D funds to technology transfer. While this falls short of the recommended amount, it is a step in the right direction. No effort has yet been made to give corporations tax incentives for sharing their technologies.

More is needed than budget allocations and tax incentives, however. To increase the flow of technology to small business, a well-defined technology transfer system must be established and implemented. Control Data offers two such systems, Technotec and Worldtech. Technotec is a commercially available computer-based information storage and retrieval network; its memory holds massive amounts of information about technologies that can be quickly recalled. Worldtech is a marketing service that gives subscribers assistance in finding, transferring, and applying specific technologies. One method of transfer involves the establishment of small companies based on replicable technologies in fields including microcircuitry, small-scale agriculture, and food processing.

There are resources besides technology that are not being wisely used. Huge reservoirs of untapped management and professional expertise exist in both big business and universities. Most small businesses urgently require professional and management consulting help, especially during start-up and the early years. Although several consulting programs already exist under the sponsorship of government agencies, local chambers of commerce, universities, and other organizations, these tend to be sporadic, not easily accessible, and not specific enough. A far better approach would be for business, universities, and community-based organizations to work together to develop a systematic method of delivering consulting and other support services to small business.

Since big business is the largest single source of persons qualified to do consulting work, it is especially important for it to recognize the profit potential inherent in aiding small companies. That this is not mere theory has been demonstrated by Control Data's success with a variety of approaches, including Business Advisors, Inc., Control Data Business Centers, and Control Data Business and Technology Centers.

Business Advisors, Inc. (BAI) was organized in 1979 to provide professional assistance to small enterprises in the areas of finance, technology management, manufacturing and processing, communications, marketing, personnel, operations, and strategic and business planning. It is unique with respect to quality, diversity, and affordability. The majority of the people involved are Control Data employees who are made available to small businesses on a part-time, temporary basis. Information about them and their specific skills is entered in a computerized "skills data bank." Also listed are the names and capabilities of retired persons and university personnel who have indicated their interest in and availability for consulting work. This arrangement has proved beneficial to all concerned: to small businesses that obtain the consulting help they need; to Control Data employees who offer their services and find

The Business and Technology Centers provide small businesses with various combinations of consulting services and facilities.

that the challenging, varied assignments give them additional expertise and wider perspectives; and to retired persons and university personnel who are given better exposure in the marketplace for their services.

Control Data Business Centers are found in urban areas throughout the United States. Small-business owners and entrepreneurs can come to the Business Centers for PLATO education and training courses; for the services of BAI, Technotec, and Worldtech; for a complete range of financial, insurance, and leasing services, including referrals to Control Data's small business investment companies; and for a choice of software and maintenance facilities for small computers and auxiliary equipment.

The Business and Technology Centers (BTCs) provide small businesses with various combinations of consulting services and facilities. Each BTC is a large building or cluster of buildings containing flexible office and laboratory space which is subdivided and leased to small companies. In addition, tenants have access to on-site information centers; drafting, accounting, purchasing, and clerical services; and a complete range of computer-based services, including PLATO, Technotec, and Worldtech.

Economies of scale make it possible for the BTCs to offer their occupants and small businesses located nearby an array of high-quality facilities and services that most would be unable to acquire on their own. Occupants also benefit substantially from the enhanced environment for peer interchange.

The first BTC opened in St. Paul, Minnesota, in 1979. This was followed by a second in Minneapolis in 1981, and others are planned for Toledo, Philadelphia, Baltimore, and San Antonio.

Control Data also provides several sources of financing for small business. Control Data Capital Corporation supplies long-term investment capital in the $100,000-$500,000 range and cooperates with other investors when larger amounts are needed. Control Data Community Ventures Fund, Inc. is licensed by the Small Business Administration to furnish long-term financing to small businesses that are at least 51 percent minority owned. Control Data Financial and Human Resources Fund, Inc. is a "high-risk" fund that provides seed money to assist in the start-up of technically oriented small businesses. And Commercial Credit Business Loans, Inc. offers several types of financing, including revolving loans secured by accounts receivable or inventories, and short-term loans secured by machinery and equipment, real estate, and other fixed assets.

We are helping small businesses to meet yet another need: employee training and education. Most large corporations have training budgets; many small companies do not. PLATO offers relevant, high-quality, easily accessible low-cost courses that persons in small business can take at times convenient to them. Several courses have been designed to improve the competence of employees; these include basic remedial instruction in reading, mathematics, and language. A number of courses have been developed specifically for small business and cover topics ranging from selling to interpreting financial statements, inventory control, cash management, short-term financing, problem analysis, and decision-making. One course, "Building Your Own Business," is of particular value to small-business owners or managers who are starting new companies or expanding existing operations. Other courses have been tailored for women entrepreneurs. PLATO is available at Control Data Learning Centers in most major cities.

In keeping with our basic tenet that the resources needed by small business can be effectively mobilized by community-based organizations, we have sponsored three projects in Minnesota which may serve as models for replication in other states: the Minnesota Cooperation Office, the Minnesota Seed Capital Fund, Inc., and the Microelectronics and Information Sciences Center. Together they make up the Minnesota Network for Small Business Innovation and Job Creation.

The Minnesota Cooperation Office (MCO) was established to foster the start-up and growth of small enterprises. It is a community-based non-profit corporation that is currently financed by contributions and grants; it is planned that it will eventually become self-supporting through a combination of client fees and funds generated by investments in client companies.

The MCO consists of a board of directors comprised of leaders from all major sectors of the community; a small permanent staff; and a voluntary advisory panel of engineers, scientists, and executives. The underlying premise is simple: an entrepreneur has an idea for a new product or service and wants to start a company, and the MCO helps to develop a business plan and obtain financing. Four "resource banks" within the MCO contain information about the following: (1) business opportunities and product ideas which can lead to the creation of new businesses; (2) entrepreneurs who can be matched with the business opportunities; (3) consultants who can provide a broad array of technical and business expertise; and (4) sources of capital for start-up ventures—the hardest type of capital to find.

The Minnesota Seed Capital Fund (MSCF) was formed because capital from more conventional sources, such as venture capital companies and banks, is often not available to new high-technology companies during their formative and developmental stages. Unlike the MCO, the MSCF is capitalized at $5 million, with stock provided primarily by larger companies, and is a for-profit venture. It offers entrepreneurs more financing possibilities than can be found in any other state.

Finally, the Microelectronics and Information Science Center (MISC) is a collaborative industry-university effort based at the University of Minnesota. Spearheaded by Control Data and funded by industry and the federal government, its objectives are to increase the amount of R&D in pivotal areas and—equally important—facilitate the commercialization of the technology generated.

Equipment and facilities are shared by industry and the university. Initial funding is $5 million, with the promise of another $5 million to come. Even though a major part of the industry funding comes from big business, small business will have equal access to the results of the R&D. It is expected that many new companies will be spawned as a result of the MISC.

In essence, the Minnesota Network for Small Business Innovation and Job Creation is a full-service agency for small businesses. It provides the support needed for each major link in what we term the "small business chain of success": technology, financing, management assistance, education, training, marketing, and efficient access to facilities and services. Without help in these areas, most small businesses are doomed to failure. The establishment of similar networks throughout the United States would certainly reduce the casualty rate of new businesses. If appropriate legislation is enacted, and if big business comes to realize that attractive profits are to be made from cooperation with small companies, the network will be replicated.

We can no longer ignore the needs of small business. Since 1974, when I became involved with the late Senator Hubert Humphrey and the passage of the Humphrey-Hawkins Act, I have grown to appreciate how valuable small business is to our economy and our way of life and how much potential exists for big businesses that are willing to get involved. I have worked continually to develop programs to encourage the start-up and growth of small enterprises. I have met with business and community leaders, devoted a great deal of time to studying the problems of small business, and attended Congressional committee hearings on the subject. Along the way, Control Data has made substantial expenditures in developing and marketing services tailored for small businesses.

We will continue to act alone and in cooperation with other corporations, government agencies, and universities to increase the success rate for new businesses and to ensure the profitable growth of existing ones. Thus far, helping small businesses has proved worthwhile and gives every indication of providing us with a lucrative customer base for as far into the future as we can imagine. Above all, we are confident that the efforts we are making will add materially to the strength and vitality of the American economy as a whole.

6

Urban Revitalization

Urban blight and urban decay have turned many of America's inner cities into breeding grounds for fear, anger, poverty, and despair. Residents are trapped in communities where there are too few jobs, where housing is substandard and medical facilities are inadequate, where businesses fail and crime is rampant. During recent decades, a number of urban revitalization programs aimed at healing our cities and reversing their steady and inexorable decline have come and gone. Although these programs have meant well, the majority of them—particularly those managed by the public sector—have been badly fragmented and crisis-reactive, devoid of long-range planning and lacking in creative risk-taking.

No urban renewal effort, however massive, could begin to solve all of the social and economic problems of our cities overnight. But any such effort will fall far short of what is needed unless it begins with and is fueled by public-private cooperation.

Over the past several years, Control Data has worked closely with government agencies and community-based organizations to formulate and implement a comprehensive approach to urban revitalization. Our involvement is based on three underlying premises:

First, that the task of building and rebuilding our cities

SOURCES

"Harnessing Technology for Better Urban Living" address (also published as part of a technology booklet series), 18th Annual Business Day Luncheon of the School of Business, University of Minnesota, Minneapolis, Minnesota, April 16, 1978.

"Technology for the Inner City—Experience and Promise" address (also published as part of a technology booklet series), Chicago United Consortium, Chicago, Illinois, September 1, 1978.

"Urban and Agricultural Problems" address, Congressional Symposium, Washington, D.C., May 4, 1979.

"Choices for Cities in the 80's" address, National League of Cities Annual Congress, Atlanta, Georgia, December 1, 1980.

presents a unique opportunity to establish a new growth industry, comparable in scope to the automobile industry in the early years of this century. There is enormous profit potential inherent in urban revitalization; responding to this major social need makes good business sense.

Second, that the major initiative, leadership, and management for a successful urban renewal program must come from business acting in cooperation with government and other sectors of society. Historically, cities have been very reluctant to adopt innovative or experimental alternatives to traditional methods and procedures. In contrast, business and industry have devoted considerable time and effort to testing and R&D. In other words, business is accustomed to taking risks, to formulating plans that extend far into the future, and to assembling diverse resources; cities are not.

Third, that any plan for building or rebuilding a community must focus on the need to provide adequate education, training, and jobs for residents. Unless these elements are emphasized from the beginning, the results are fated to be little more than cosmetic.

The centerpiece of our approach to urban revitalization is a consortium called City Venture Corporation. Organized in the summer of 1978, City Venture markets its services to communities, cities, states, and federal agencies. Capitalized at $3 million, it is not prepared to fund any large-scale developments, but it will, where appropriate, invest in innovative projects and private businesses with advanced technologies applicable to urban development. Its income does not come from property ownership or the appreciation of land values, but instead is derived from fees for the initiation, planning, and management of comprehensive urban renewal programs.

Numbered among City Venture's original 15 stockholders were two religious organizations, the American Lutheran Church and the United Church of Christ, and 12 corporations in addition to Control Data, including Bertrand Goldberg Associates, Honeywell, Medtronic, the Minneapolis Star and Tribune Company, the Northwest Bancorporation, First Bank Systems, Inc., and Reynolds

Metals. That two religious organizations agreed to participate was a landmark event that contributed to the consortium's acceptability and indicated its desire to heed the
rights and needs of individuals and seek a balance between
profitability and social responsibility.

Until City Venture was formed, there was no entity
capable of developing and implementing a holistic long-
term solution to the formidable problems of our inner
cities. No serious, large-scale utilization of available and
emerging technologies had ever been attempted. There had
been little long-range planning and virtually no creative or
experimental risk-taking. No forum had existed in which
the private sector could work in partnership with the public
sector to generate shared solutions. And the economic opportunities presented by urban revitalization had been ignored.

The consortium has as its philosophy the belief that the
act of building and rebuilding American cities can be a
profitable growth enterprise. It concentrates primarily on
blighted and stagnated inner-city communities because
their problems are the most acute and pervasive; however,
its approach can and should be extended to other communities as well, since the problems they face usually differ
only in degree.

City Venture focuses on meeting two basic needs: the
need for high-quality, accessible, affordable education and
training; and, even more important, the need for jobs. No
program for urban renewal can be successful unless it provides job opportunities for community residents and training programs to enable people to get and keep the jobs
which are created. Without adequate employment, a re-
built area will only deteriorate again when people are
unable to pay rent, buy or maintain homes, or purchase
health care, food, or transportation services.

By emphasizing training, education, and jobs, City Venture does not deny that housing and other community
needs are also important. Rather, it asserts that these needs
can only be met effectively if education and jobs are made
available first. Programs that begin by addressing these
other needs—in other words, by taking the "bricks-and-
mortar" approach—have proved to be insufficient and

short-lived. The "education and jobs" method requires
holistic planning and the gathering of extensive and frequently scattered resources, and thus is somewhat elusive
and difficult to implement, but it does work.

City Venture also encourages and assists in the establishment of small businesses in target areas. Small businesses
are a major source of jobs and have a significant effect on
the building, rebuilding, and maintenance of commercial
centers and housing. They provide health care, education,
and social services, together with a myriad of other essential products and services ranging from food production,
processing and distribution, to waste recycling. In addition, they give their employees a sense of having control
over their lives and their communities, and offer them economic opportunities and incentives. A community founded on a base of diverse and plentiful small enterprises is
more self-sufficient and responsive to its residents' changing needs than one that is dependent upon a few large companies and a host of public programs.

From the outset, City Venture has viewed urban renewal
as a total process. Integral to this process is the ongoing
assembling of a broad range of technologies drawn from
the physical and social sciences. These include technologies
relating to employment and management; energy-efficient
construction; less costly sources of energy; advanced
waste-recycling methods; improvements in the quality,
equality, and the productivity of education; urban agriculture; transportation; and health care. Most of the new and
emerging technologies that could be used for revitalizing
cities are found within large corporations; until now, most
have been underutilized or inaccessible to outsiders. City
Venture is working to bring them together and make them
more readily available to people and organizations that
need them.

Cities across the country have long been hesitant to
adopt creative or experimental alternatives to the traditional methods of meeting urban needs. Many of these
alternatives are embodied in existing and emerging technologies. If it were possible to build a model city incorporating these technologies, their effectiveness would be

demonstrated on a large scale, and this would no doubt stimulate a widespread program of urban revitalization. But the costs of developing such a city would be prohibitive; the best estimates suggest that, in order for results to be conclusive, it would have to consist of around 1,000 households and would run somewhere around $200 million to build. Even if by some stretch of the imagination financing for a model city were to become available, it would take at least a decade or more before any meaningful evaluation could be conducted. We could not afford to wait that long.

Many of the technologies that could be used to facilitate urban revitalization are already at hand; one of the most obvious is computerized information storage and retrieval. With assistance from the National League of Cities, the National Association of Counties, and the Council for International Urban Liaison, Control Data has developed two data base services, the Urban Technology Exchange (UTE) and the Local Government Information Network (LOGIN). UTE contains information on economic development programs and ways to create jobs, and is used primarily by businesses. LOGIN is intended for local governments and municipalities, and contains information on productivity improvement, capital facilities maintenance, energy management, and housing retrofit and renovation. The systems also function as communications networks through which users can exchange data on-line.

There is no reason why this concept could not be used to address other needs as well, especially in the area of human services. An example of this type of application would be a computerized data base for the immediate retrieval of information about health care, housing, child care, counseling, and jobs. In the past, many human services have been made available through government bureaus, but little attention has been paid to avoiding the duplication of efforts or determining marketplaces. A decentralized delivery system responsive to individuals could enhance the vitality of entire communities and create a new spectrum of professional and paraprofessional jobs for residents.

Other technologies that could be applied to urban renewal on a broad scale are those relating to energy-efficient construction. Control Data has built two energy-efficient facilities in St. Paul: a small office and apartment building called Terratech, and a World Distribution Center. Terratech is earth-sheltered and uses solar energy, waste recycling, and other energy-saving technologies. The World Distribution Center is the largest solar-energy equipment industrial facility in the United States and is 45 percent earth-sheltered. Substantial benefits have been realized from the earth-sheltering alone; during a week of sub-zero temperatures and strong winds in the winter of 1980-81, the World Distribution Center consumed only one-fourth as much heating oil as did a more conventionally built and comparably sized CDC building located nearby.

Through UTE, LOGIN, and energy-efficient construction, Control Data is demonstrating that various technologies can be used to solve some of the problems of our cities. But technology alone, no matter how sophisticated or how well applied, cannot provide all of the answers. Also needed are human resources—people with special skills and areas of expertise.

City Venture draws upon a wide range of human resources. Many managers and other professionals within large companies are relatively unchallenged for a good part of their time, and studies have found that they cannot work continuously on one type of problem and remain productive. City Venture offers managers and other professionals the chance to participate on a part-time or, for limited periods, full-time basis in urban renewal projects. This arrangement is beneficial to corporate personnel, who grow through exposure to new ideas and the opportunity to apply their skills in new ways; to the consortium, which has access to the wealth of knowledge and expertise they bring; and to the cities that contract with City Venture.

The success of any City Venture undertaking relies heavily on community participation and support—not only from leaders from a particular neighborhood for which a given project is planned, but also from leaders from businesses in the community and from county, city, and state government offices. As a policy, City Venture will not initiate a project unless a formally structured means of gaining access to community resources and support is present. Obviously, matters are greatly simplified when one jurisdiction has the authority to act for most of the citizens involved; this is seldom the case, however. In any event, the fact that City Venture is a consortium unburdened by the vested interests associated with single organizations helps it to gain consensus among whatever jurisdictions may be present.

City Venture has made considerable progress since it was first launched in 1978. Contracts have been signed with the cities of Toledo; Philadelphia; Baltimore; Charleston, South Carolina; Benton Harbor and Saginaw, Michigan; and San Antonio. Negotiations are currently under way with a number of other cities.

In Toledo, where City Venture has been present for about two years, its ultimate goal is the creation of 2,000 new jobs and the revitalization of a depressed 280-acre area within the Warren-Sherman community. In recent years, unemployment in Warren-Sherman has exceeded 32 percent; housing has been inadequate, rundown, or burned out; residents have been poorly educated, ill-trained, and at the lower reaches of the economic scale; and commercial and recreational facilities and small businesses have been almost nonexistent.

During the past two years, the area has been awarded federal, state, and local government grants and investments totaling $12 million and has received commitments from the private sector amounting to $34.5 million. Work has commenced on a 23-acre industrial park that will provide off-street parking and sites for industrial and commercial operations. A Control Data Business and Technology Center (BTC) that anchors the park has already been completed; thus far, its tenants include Control Data personnel, a Fair Break training facility, four new minority-owned businesses, and a manufacturing operation owned by Magnetic Peripherals, Inc. Ground has been broken for a 4.5-acre shopping center that will house a dozen commercial and retail establishments. A Toledo Trust Branch Bank and Professional Building is scheduled to be built across the street from the shopping center, and Owens-

Illinois has begun construction of a plant in the industrial park. Most recently a local contractor, encouraged by the presence of $1.2 million earmarked for interest subsidies for home purchases, has started to improve the housing stock in the neighborhood through a combination of rehabilitation projects and new construction.

In Baltimore, City Venture is working in the Park Heights neighborhood. A typical City Venture target area, it has a high minority population—82 percent black—and a substantial unemployment rate—40 percent in 1978. Its residents are on the average poorly educated and have received little job training.

Efforts in Park Heights are in a large part the result of a four-party agreement among the City of Baltimore, the Baltimore Economic Development Corporation, the Park Heights Development Corporation, and City Venture. Together they have set two objectives: stimulating business growth within Park Heights, and creating some 2,500 new jobs over a five-year period. Plans call for the installation of a Control Data BTC, a Fair Break facility, and a PLATO learning center; the preparation of low-cost space in existing buildings for manufacturing and commercial operations; and new construction on some 47 acres previously designated for future industrial development.

Despite its conspicuous achievements in Toledo, Baltimore, and other cities, City Venture has encountered difficulties in some areas, most notably in Control Data's home city of Minneapolis. When we initiated our first project here in 1979, misunderstandings arose among the consortium, local government, and local community groups which eventually led to our terminating a project to rehabilitate a blighted area contiguous to the city's new Metrodome development. That experience taught us how important it is to get all participants involved from the outset, even if doing so takes time and occasions delays.

Although City Venture's major plan for Minneapolis was not realized, the project did result in some significant job-creation programs in the neighborhood. A Control Data Business and Technology Center was built, and a Control Data Bindery was opened. The Bindery currently

*Most recently, a local contractor. . . has started to improve
the housing stock in the neighborhood through a combination of rehabilitation projects and new construction.*

provides part-time employment for 54 persons — a majority of whom are American Indians — who cannot work full-time because of school schedules or other considerations. The Business and Technology Center, which has been operational for over a year, provides space and services to new and growing small businesses; it is anticipated that these small businesses will in turn generate several hundred new jobs within the community during the coming years.

In the Liberty City area of Miami, City Venture was initially engaged to design a plan to rehabilitate the community. After accepting the plan, city and local business groups decided to implement it themselves rather than contracting with City Venture to do so. That the program is under way is more important than who is doing the implementing; by serving as a catalyst, City Venture was instrumental in bringing into being a well-conceived approach to community improvement which might otherwise never have taken shape.

The consortium had other concrete effects on Liberty City. A Fair Break center is now operational there and working overtime; the first new business has opened; 250 area residents have been placed in jobs as a direct result of City Venture efforts; and two additional new businesses will begin operating once the necessary seed capital money becomes available.

In Minneapolis and Liberty City, City Venture did not achieve all of its goals. But it did achieve some of them, and this alone is remarkable considering the sensitive, deep-seated, and complex problems with which it was attempting to deal.

It is unrealistic to expect that every City Venture project will proceed smoothly. Each community has its own local organizations, many of which may have plans and programs of their own in mind. Their leaders may feel threatened by City Venture or, for that matter, by any group that comes in from the outside. City Venture operates in a political milieu, and jurisdictional interests together with political ambitions often present obstacles to the consensus which is necessary for program authorization and funding. Sometimes it is possible to surmount these obstacles; sometimes it is not. We are not discouraged by the fact that in a few instances the end results of our efforts have fallen short of our hopes. Instead, we are encouraged by what we have managed to accomplish thus far.

In cities like Toledo and Baltimore, City Venture has proved to be an effective vehicle for dealing with the complex problems of deteriorating urban communities. Its presence gives credence to the feasibility of public-private cooperation and opens the door to similar efforts in blighted communities across the country. It is planned that the consortium will eventually be profitable; if it is not, it will simply be perceived as yet another low-cost, "do-gooder" effort on the part of a group of large companies. While participants cannot expect significant returns on their investments in the early years, especially when City Venture is compared to their other profit sources, a responsible rate of return over the long term is the goal of all concerned.

We expect that other large companies will join City Venture primarily because of the opportunity it offers them to sell their products and services in previously unexplored markets. Companies specializing in communications, education, health care, waste reclamation, alternative energy sources, low-cost building components, energy-efficient construction methods, small-scale food processing, and urban agriculture stand to gain the most from participation in the consortium. City Venture also gives companies a way to address some of our society's most urgent needs — a responsibility that can no longer be ignored.

There are tremendous resources within the private sector that can and must be put to use for urban renewal and revitalization. City Venture has demonstrated that these can be channeled into profit-making endeavors and, in the process, make a major contribution to improving the equality of life in the disadvantaged areas of our urban communities.

7

Rural Revitalization

In the past 50 years, large-scale agriculture in the United States has developed into a booming business, but at great cost. Little regard has been paid to the resulting loss of jobs, damage to the environment, harmful effects on human health, and depletion of future production capacity caused by practices that are equivalent to mining the soil. Many of the so-called efficiencies of modern-day farming have been achieved at society's expense through subsidies to agribusiness provided by government and universities. So much attention has been given to improving and further expanding large farms that the needs of small family farms have essentially been ignored; as a consequence, America's small farms are in deep trouble.

Leveling a broad indictment at the community of large farmers and their supporters will not solve this dilemma. Rather, we must make constructive changes in large-scale farming practices and focus once again on smaller operations. And we must do so in spite of the prevailing view: namely, that small farms have no profit potential.

SOURCES

"Back to the Countryside via Technology" address (also published as part of a technology booklet series), National Agri-Marketing Outlook Conference, Kansas City, Missouri, November 8, 1977.

"Technology for the Small Farm and Food Processor" address, Appalachian Land Festival, Clarksburg, West Virginia, October 28, 1978.

"Small Rural Enterprise" address, luncheon for Archbishop John Roach, President, National Conference of Catholic Bishops, Washington, D.C., April 23, 1979. (Also presented at a luncheon for Atherton Bean, Chairman of the Executive Committee for International Multifoods, Minneapolis, Minnesota, September 13, 1979; and at a Land O'Lakes dinner, Washington, D.C., September 18, 1979.)

"Rural Venture—The Small Farms Component" audiovisual presentation, September 1980.

"Responding to the Technological Challenges of Small Scale Agriculture" address (also published as part of a technology booklet series), Special Symposium on Research for Small Farms, Beltsville, Maryland, November 17, 1981.

Most experts agree that social benefits would be derived from improving the lot of the small farmer, but few believe that small farms could yield attractive economic benefits or become significant contributors to the food chain. There is a growing body of evidence that the so-called experts are wrong and that better solutions to many of the basic problems plaguing the nation's food chain could be found by ensuring the survival of the small family farm.

A 1981 USDA *Report on the Economies of Size in U.S. Field Crop Farming* concludes that "farms reach efficiency at small or modest sizes" and that "many commercial farms now exceed the size necessary to achieve all available cost efficiencies." The study further states that "since medium-size commercial farms with gross incomes from $41,000 to $76,000 achieve most technical cost efficiencies, society benefits little in terms of lower real food costs from further increases in farm size." In other words, small family farms may have more to offer over the longer term than large, capital-intensive, fossil fuel-based operations.

To me, the most convincing evidence of the need to reverse the trend toward large-scale agriculture stems from what I saw as a boy growing up on a farm in Nebraska. At that time, most farms were around 160 acres in size, and both crops and livestock were raised. Horsepower and organic fertilizers were used, and the farms were self-sufficient to a high degree; the net result was that both they and the small towns nearby prospered.

With the introduction of fossil-fuel, capital-intensive, less integrated farming methods, the self-sufficiency of farms decreased dramatically. Profitability declined because a larger portion of each farm's proceeds was shared with agribusiness. And that in turn triggered the consolidation of small farms into larger ones. More and more people left the land, striking the death knell for many small towns in rural America. Not only did I witness the family farm's struggle to survive in the midst of change; I saw the passing of a way of life integral to our heritage.

Past experience, current practices, and numerous experiments support the proposition that small-scale farms and food processors can be made viable once again. Models have demonstrated substantial production gains following the integration of limited acreage high-value crops and small-scale animal agriculture, most notably sheep and hog farming. Corresponding models are being developed for dairy goats and beef cattle. In Denmark, the Netherlands, Korea, and Japan—countries which have a preponderance of small farms—intensive agriculture is resulting in higher yields per acre for a variety of crops. In the eastern United States, a number of innovative farmers have found that utilizing selected intercropping of from two to eight plant varieties not only reduces soil erosion, but also increases profits by close to 50 percent.

New solar technologies, irrigation methods, wind generation, small-scale machinery, and controlled-environment crop growing can all be applied to small-scale farming with excellent results. In-hand and emerging solar technologies can improve the efficiency of small-scale grain drying and storage as well as provide sources of power for irrigation and adequate heating for animal buildings, even in northern climates.

Tests conducted on a small-scale sprinkler irrigation system, currently nearing completion, indicate a 15 percent savings in energy and as much as a 20 percent savings in water—statistics that are encouraging in light of the fact that water tables are declining and wells are drying in many areas of the United States. Wind generators in the range of the 10-25KW will soon be cost-effective and represent a significant step toward farm energy self-sufficiency. Machines designed for small-scale farming—including tractors, tillage implements, harvesters, and sophisticated human-propelled tools—are becoming more readily available. And small-scale controlled-environment agriculture, in which light, heat, atmosphere, nutrients, and other environmental factors affecting plant life are closely regulated, is resulting in much higher production per unit of space.

Many additional technologies could be mentioned, but these examples aptly illustrate that we have sufficient know-how to enhance the productivity of small family farms and small-scale food processors. It stands to reason that further R&D will more firmly establish increased viability over a wider range of conditions.

Control Data has engaged in a multifaceted program designed to revitalize the agrarian sector of the economy through improvements in small-scale farming. The rationale for our decision is simply that with proper selection and application of emerging technologies, and with ongoing R&D, small farms and small-scale food-processing operations can reduce food costs, make a sizable contribution to food production, do so in ways that are more protective of the environment, and provide a decent living for their owners.

We realize that these objectives will not be achieved immediately, but we do believe that sufficient technology exists to enable us to get meaningful results within a few years. And, with adequate and continuing support, we feel that these results can become significant on a national scale in ten to fifteen years. In the process, we expect that Control Data will earn a reasonable profit from investments in these and related efforts.

Specifically, we are (1) assembling a computer data base containing information on existing and emerging technologies appropriate to small-scale farming; (2) catalyzing further R&D relative to small-scale technologies; (3) preparing educational and training materials so that high-quality, easily available, and affordable education and training can be offered to small-scale farmers; (4) establishing Control Data-owned and locally owned and operated Agriculture and Business Service Centers (ABCs) for the distribution of technology, education and training, and other services to persons operating small farms and related small businesses; and (5) participating in Rural Ventures, a consortium dedicated to increasing the productivity and profitability of small farms.

In cooperation with a worldwide group of experts, Control Data is compiling a computer data base of agricultural technologies called Agtech. Thus far, it includes practical information on crop and livestock production; alternative energy sources such as wind, solar, and biomass energy; more efficient irrigation methods; and other topics of value to small-scale farmers. The listings are presented in straightforward "how-to" language, and are directed toward answering often-asked questions such as: "What are the nutritional requirements for baby feeder pigs?" "How can the summer milk-production slump in dairy cows be avoided?" and "How can I recognize potato blight?" Agtech has been growing steadily since it was begun in 1979; by 1985, it will contain more than 30,000 units of information, all brief and to the point.

To stimulate R&D in the area of small-scale agriculture and support the development of small-scale technologies, Control Data has for a number of years awarded grants to universities and research institutes. Examples include grants to the University of Minnesota for work on low-investment swine production and to Purdue University for work on small-scale forage crop systems. In addition, we have acted on the belief that demonstrating success will encourage R&D on the part of others by providing direct assistance to small-scale farms in incorporating applicable technologies. Some of the technologies currently being used are fluid drill planting, seed pregermination, expandable plastic mulch, solar grain drying, warm water/milk heat exchangers, earth berming, residential biomass heating, and passive solar heating.

We are investing in small-scale food processing, in small companies that manufacture products needed by small farmers, and in small-scale controlled-environment agriculture. For example, we have invested in Fisher Foods of Princeton, Minnesota, and in Jacobs Electric Company of Plymouth, Minnesota. Fisher makes prepared soups and salads, and purchases much of its produce from local farmers. Jacobs has developed and is marketing a highly reliable 10KW wind generator suitable for use in widely differing geographic locations; progress is being made on 15KW and 25KW models.

On the roof of cne of our own company buildings in Minneapolis, we have installed a greenhouse for the purpose of studying one type of controlled-environment agriculture. The greenhouse uses both natural and artificial lighting, and is heated by waste heat from large computers on the floor below it. A small computer installed on the premises regulates the temperature and the amount of carbon dioxide in the air. Another facility located on the roof is totally enclosed and utilizes only artificial lighting; in it we are experimenting with multiponics. These technologies are usable in virtually all parts of the world and are being franchised.

Our primary vehicle for providing education and training to farmers is PLATO, Control Data's computer-based education system. More than 1,000 hours of agriculture lessons are being prepared; courses vary from six to 47 hours in length and are designed to permit users to select only the information they really need. Courseware already available covers topics ranging from sheep production and management to small-farm orientation, starting to farm, beekeeping, woodlot management, feeder pig production and management, fuel woodyard management, the use of livestock guard dogs, and rural energy concept sources. Special attention has been given to courses devoted to basic management principles and techniques. These include instruction in accounting, the application of least-cost production methods, the fundamentals of crop and livestock selection, performance measurement, and the maintenance of livestock production schedules.

PLATO also offers basic skills and high school skills curricula. These are especially important to the advancement of small-scale agriculture in poverty-stricken rural areas of developing countries, where many persons are functionally illiterate.

We believe that the computer—and programs like PLATO and Agtech—are essential to the success of small-scale farming. Without it, relevant technologies will not be efficiently assembled and distributed, and education and training will prove too costly. We are continuing to explore additional ways in which computers and computer data bases can be used to benefit small farms and address their specific needs.

Control Data Agricultural and Business Service Centers (ABCs), the rural counterparts of our urban Business and Technology Centers (BTCs), will play a key role in our agrarian revitalization program. The first ABC was opened in Princeton, Minnesota, in 1980. Staffed by Control Data personnel, the Princeton center offers access to both Agtech and PLATO, and provides members of the local

Computers and computer data bases can be used to benefit small farms and address their specific needs.

community with assistance in the preparation of small farm and business plans and the selection of appropriate technologies; information about new products and production aids; and help in analyzing financial and production data.

Every rural community needs an agricultural center of some type. We anticipate that locally owned and operated ABCs, operating under licensing agreements, will evolve into increasingly attractive small business opportunities as Agtech grows and more PLATO courses become available. It will be possible, for example, to start a small center with an initial capital investment of under $15,000—an amount sufficient to purchase a small computer, selected education and training courses, and telephone access to Agtech.

In addition to working independently on a number of rural revitalization projects, Control Data is active in Rural Ventures, Inc., a for-profit consortium established in 1979. Rural Ventures was begun with 18 shareholders, including Control Data and three other corporations; two agricultural cooperatives; a foundation; five religious groups; a health service organization; several individuals; and the Institute of Cultural Affairs.

The consortium aims to increase the productivity and profitability of small farms by assisting in the start-up and growth of small businesses in rural communities. It contracts with individuals and groups to prepare farm business plans, provides a variety of consulting services, and draws upon Control Data training programs tailored to individual needs. It also focuses on improving education and training, health care, housing, and communications in depressed rural areas, and on creating new jobs.

Rural Ventures has already made excellent progress. Its first project, headquartered at Pine City, Minnesota, was originally financed entirely by Control Data and started in the spring of 1979. The 18 farmers who participated had experience ranging from zero to ten years; many had failed to achieve more than limited success prior to their involvement in the program. Their farms varied in size from five to 140 acres and were located on marginal land in an area considered by the government to be economically depressed.

When the Pine City program began, all 18 participants were part-time farmers. Within a year, several were able to quit their off-farm jobs and support themselves by farming full time. There is good reason to expect that most of the others will eventually reach the point where they can do the same.

A second Rural Ventures project financed by Control Data was started in 1980 in Princeton, Minnesota, with a group of 15 beginning farmers. Its main objective is to establish viable operations which can be widely replicated. The target farms are 80 to 140 acres in size, and the land is somewhat better than that in the Pine City project area. Unlike the Pine City participants, most of the Princeton farmers are new to the land.

Rural Ventures provides a number of support services to Princeton farmers, including access to appropriate technologies and PLATO courses through an ABC; help with the design and construction of farm buildings; and aid in obtaining financing. During the first stage of the program, four passive solar, earth-sheltered homes and a variety of farm buildings were constructed. A year later, crops were planted and livestock operations begun. Rural Ventures managers who live in the vicinity are assisting in every phase of the program, and it is planned that most of the participants will soon be fully self-supporting.

Today Pine City and Princeton are part of a larger six-county Rural Ventures project in east-central Minnesota. New projects are currently under way in such diverse locations as Alaska, New England, Virginia, and Jamaica.

In Alaska, Rural Ventures has been involved since 1980 in small-scale farming and community development programs based in Ambler and Selawik, two Eskimo villages. Located above the Arctic Circle some 670 miles northwest of Anchorage and 300 miles east of the Soviet Union, they have a combined population of close to 800 in a region with a total population of approximately 5,500.

Ambler is the site of an integrated small-farm operation combining vegetable and small-grain growing with livestock production. Thirty-five acres of tundra have been cleared and a variety of vegetables grown, including potatoes, turnips, carrots, lettuce, and cabbage. Test crops

In Alaska, Rural Ventures has been involved in small-scale farming and community development programs in two Eskimo villages.

of wheat, buckwheat, and rapeseed have also been planted with an eye toward providing feed grains for later herds of sheep, goats, or reindeer. All of the crops selected have short growing seasons. A second farm is in operation in Selawik. The Ambler farm is managed by an Eskimo and his wife; the Selawik farm is currently run by the village as a community effort, but will eventually be divided among a number of individuals.

Rural Ventures's contract with the New England Regional Development Commission calls for the improvement and expansion of sheep production in a six-state area. By applying the latest technologies, the consortium expects to significantly improve the net incomes of small farmers and related businesses. During November of 1980, the first year of the program, 25 farmers from the Connecticut River Valley participated; that number will be increased to 60 by the end of October 1982.

In December of 1981, Rural Ventures completed a nine-month contract with the Virginia State Private Industry Council to develop a plan for creating private-sector jobs within a ten-county area during the next five years. The plan submitted consists of three major components: agricultural development, small business development, and job preparation training. The major emphasis is on agriculture, specifically diversified small-scale operations. The ultimate objective is to provide services to several hundred small farmers that will enable them to derive a decent income from full-time farming and, in turn, hire more workers.

Finally, a new Rural Ventures consortium is being formed in Jamaica to work with Rural Ventures in the United States on applying small-scale farming technologies to the needs of some 150,000 small- and medium-scale Jamaican farmers. Since the election of a new government in 1980, Jamaica has begun turning away from socialism and toward an emphasis on private enterprise. Prime Minister Edward Seaga has appealed to the Reagan administration for assistance, and one result has been the establishment of the U.S. Business Committee on Jamaica, of which I am a member. Together we have agreed that agriculture will be a primary area for aggressive development.

Rural Ventures will provide a vehicle for disseminating technologies, information, and training.

Although significant advances have been made to date in small-scale farming, they are modest compared to what can and should be done. Control Data's own programs, as well as the achievements of Rural Ventures, have clearly demonstrated the potential inherent in small-scale farming, but efforts must be greatly accelerated if we are to meet a number of pressing business, economic, and social needs both here and overseas.

Many people simply do not realize the seriousness of the problems America's farmers are experiencing. They look instead at statistics touting the productivity of farming in the United States: statistics showing that one American farm worker currently produces enough food for himself and some 60 other people, and that during the 1970s one-third of our total agricultural output was exported—a ratio of export-to-production never achieved by any other country. They fail to see the broad picture. The profitability of American agriculture is in fact anemic and propped up by government subsidies. Yields of major food crops have plateaued, and the yield per acre is actually higher in many other countries where small farms are predominant. And the adverse effects of large-scale, fossil-fuel, capital-intensive agriculture on jobs, the environment, and human health have not been sufficiently or intelligently evaluated.

We must stimulate growth in agricultural production, both to meet rising world food demands and to help correct massive U.S. foreign trade deficits. This will require increased levels of crop yields and/or the dedication of more land, energy, and water to farming. Genetic improvements, greater photosynthetic efficiency, the enhancement of nitrogen-fixing capabilities, and other methods revealed by further R&D will no doubt increase crop yields. But the promise these new technologies hold must be put into proper perspective: it takes at least a decade before a given technology can be moved out of the research laboratory and onto a farm.

Turning more land, energy, and water over to farming poses another set of dilemmas. Urban sprawl consumes from one- to two-million acres of previously cultivated land per year. Continued soil erosion is steadily decreasing the productivity of our best farm land. It may be possible to utilize currently uncultivated marginal land, but not if we persist with large-scale fossil-fuel intensive farming methods. Lands that offer the greatest potential for small-scale agriculture include the arid regions of the western United States; huge uncultivated areas of Alaska; and underutilized acreages on Indian reservations. Each will require a totally different approach to farming.

Our resources are limited, and it takes time to implement new technologies. Large-scale farming has already had deleterious effects on our economy and the American way of life. These are the facts. On the positive side, we have the know-how to significantly enhance the productivity of small family farms. And that is where the answer to many of our problems lies.

The expansion of small-scale agriculture will meet other needs as well. Rural poverty in the United States is widespread. Forty percent of our nation's poor live in rural communities, and more than a quarter of them in substandard housing. Health care facilities are inadequate, especially in isolated areas; some of the worst are found on Indian reservations. Rural Ventures is in the initial stages of developing small-scale agricultural programs with a number of tribes to enhance employment and encourage economic advancement for tribal members. These programs will help, but they must be widely replicated before any real change can be effected.

Many rural areas are paralyzed by high unemployment. The lack of industry and the scarcity of capital and management and technical resources make jobs almost impossible to find. Increasing the efficiency of small-scale agriculture can provide the means for generating new jobs both on and off the farm. Studies indicate that for every job created on a farm, two more come into being in nearby small towns. These can provide career opportunities for disadvantaged youths, among others.

For the millions of small farmers in developing countries, the need for efficient small-scale agriculture is especially urgent. Per capita food production is declining in nations around the world, with the exception of parts of Asia. The progress achieved with the large-scale "green revolution" agriculture of the last half century has slowed sharply in recent years; unless significant improvements are made in small-scale agriculture, the situation will only worsen. The Rural Ventures project in Jamaica can well serve as a stepping-stone for a broader-based effort in other countries.

To accelerate the advancement of small-scale agriculture in the United States, a national program of policy changes and innovative legislation is needed. One critical change in policy would be the redirection of more federal and state research funds into small-scale technology development, particularly in the areas of integrated small-scale production and energy generation. At the present time, federal support for small-scale agriculture amounts to less than one percent of the total annual funding for agriculture-related research. The percentage is a bit higher at state levels, but it is still inadequate. Fortunately, substantially more research directly applicable to small-scale farming is being performed overseas; an international program for the exchange of technology would bring some of it home to us.

New legislation should be directed toward increasing the availability of low-cost loans to small farmers; providing tax incentives for those who sell land to small farmers; giving tax credits to persons who invest in ABCs; and encouraging the establishment of rural enterprise zones. Legislative incentives like these would cost the taxpayers money, but they would prove to be good investments over the long term because they would facilitate job creation. Estimates indicate that the cost in government funding per job created by Rural Ventures-type projects would average around $15,000; considering that the estimated value to society of a typical job is close to $52,000 each year, and that a job in the private sector tends to last for ten years or more, the returns from such one-time investments would be enormous.

A national program to stimulate job creation in rural areas by expanding small-scale agriculture is long overdue.

The question is one of who should take the initiative in planning, managing, and implementing such a program. The Department of Agriculture, the Agriculture Extension Service, universities, and federal and state governments are all laboring under traditional constraints and shrinking budgets, and it seems unlikely that they would be able to accomplish much on their own. But if the private sector were to take decisive action, both government and academia would probably respond by contributing a great deal of support and professional expertise.

A huge domestic market is developing for small-farm technologies; potential demand is high, and much progress has already been made in establishing feasibility. We know from experience that large numbers of young people are eager for careers in farming and cannot attain them under the present system: We also know that families who currently operate larger farms are unable to generate sufficient income to continue indefinitely; if current conditions persist, they will not stay in farming. The small-scale model offers attractive opportunities to both groups.

If the private sector is willing to be far-sighted enough to develop, assemble, and deliver the technologies needed to facilitate small-scale farming, it is sure to reap benefits. For example, we expect our Agricultural and Business Service Centers to play a pivotal role in our own rural revitalization program. In 1982, ten individuals who have indicated a deep personal commitment will participate with Control Data in the opening of more new ABCs. We plan to increase the number to 100 in 1983. By the end of 1988, we intend to have some 10,000 centers in operation both here and overseas.

This may seem like an overly optimistic goal, but the seriousness of the situation calls for goals we must stretch for maximum progress. America has been the world's breadbasket of last resort for more than a century, and we have continued to provide our own citizens with a stable, plentiful, and nutritious food supply on an unparalleled scale. My personal experience on the land, combined with 50 years of experience embracing a broad range of technology, has convinced me that responding to the challenges of small-scale agriculture is vital to the preservation of our heritage. Equally important, it is the only way we can approach the awesome task of improving agricultural production in developing countries. If we are to meet one of the most basic of all human needs—the need for food—we must return to the small farms of the past, bearing with us the technologies of the future.

8

Health Care

Since the early 1970s, Control Data has been active in several programs in the field of health care. Our involvement has been based on three premises: (1) that society can no longer afford the costs of today's health care system; (2) that efforts at achieving better, more affordable health care must be directed toward preventing illness rather than treating it after the fact; and (3) that the main initiative to meet this major societal need must come from business.

In many respects, we are challenging from the outside both the economics and the methods of the health care system as it currently exists. We are doing so because we believe that the provider community—the thousands of businesses that constitute our health care system—cannot realistically be expected to do the job itself. Highly fragmented and bound by a professional tradition of individual autonomy, it lacks incentives to change. The care it delivers is usually of high quality, but it is also wasteful of valuable resources. Group health insurance and other types of reimbursement arrangements reward neither the consumer nor the provider for efficiency, and thus efficiency is not a goal. As wastefulness continues, expenditures rise.

Since 1970, health care costs in the United States have escalated at nearly twice the overall inflation rate. Americans bear the highest per capita health care costs in the world, yet we do not rank among the top ten nations on most common health indices. Virtually unrestricted outlays yield at best only marginal returns. The situation will worsen if we persist in following our present course of limited intervention on the part of business and piecemeal planning on the part of government, both of which address

SOURCE

"The Pathway to Better Health via Technology" address (also published as part of a technology booklet series), Role of Wellness in the Workplace Conference, Minneapolis, Minnesota, March 30, 1979.

the symptoms and not the causes of the problem.

Even for those who can afford it, health care is not always readily accessible. For example, the United States has more doctors in proportion to its population than Sweden, the Netherlands, Finland, or France, but the U.S. doctors are less evenly distributed. In 1977, Mississippi had 1.05 active physicians per 1,000 people; New York State had 2.43. Persons who live in urban and suburban areas have an abundance of health care resources to choose from, but residents of many rural areas and some inner-city communities do not. Perhaps the greatest inequity exists on our Indian reservations, where the level of health care offered is appallingly poor.

In recognition of the need to bring adequate health care to isolated areas, Control Data embarked on its first health-related program in 1975. We began an experimental project with representatives of the Rosebud Indian Reservation, located in a remote part of South Dakota.

Prior to our involvement, one severely understaffed hospital had been responsible for the care of some 8,500 native Americans, many of whom lived up to 130 miles away from it along dirt roads. Little or no transportation to and from the hospital was available. Control Data financed and staffed a mobile clinic that traveled the reservation for four and one-half years, serving up to 900 residents per month. Today the van has been replaced by two permanent clinics run by trained Indian paramedics, and substantial progress has been made in the health of the tribe as a whole. But much more remains to be done. In response, we are using PLATO, our computer-based education and training program, to teach tribal members self-health care.

The Rosebud project not only helps those who live on the reservation, but also performs an important R&D function for us. In learning how to improve the quality of health care in this one area, we have gathered a body of knowledge that will be widely applicable and will eventually serve as the foundation for a profitable business.

The greatest inequity exists on our Indian reservations, where the level of health care is appallingly poor.... Control Data financed and staffed a mobile clinic that traveled the reservation.

As a culture, we are accustomed to treating and curing diseases, not preventing them. This is shockingly evident in the fact that of the approximately $200 billion spent annually on health care, less than 2.5 percent is spent on disease prevention and only .5 percent goes toward health education. Yet the greatest improvements in mortality and morbidity rates have resulted from improvements in public health, nutrition, and living standards. There is a clear message here, but it is not being heeded.

It should be obvious that devoting more resources to health education and illness prevention would have two parallel effects: it would make us healthier as a people, and it would reduce the skyrocketing costs of health care. Dr. Henry Blackburn, director of the Laboratory of Physiological Hygiene at the University of Minnesota, phrased it aptly when he said, "An ounce of prevention is not worth a pound of cure...there is no cure for the major maladies of modern man. Prevention is the only answer." The "major maladies of modern man" include the chronic diseases of middle and old age, primarily heart disease, cancer, and strokes. None can be "cured"; all can be prevented to a great degree.

For example, the United States government spends close to $1 billion annually to treat "black lung," an occupational disease that strikes coal miners. If appropriate measures had been taken 30 years ago, the disease could largely have been prevented. Similarly, diseases resulting from cigarette smoking, also preventable, cost more than $20 billion a year. And circulatory illnesses, about half of which could be prevented by controlling health-risk factors, cost the economy an additional $39 billion. These three expenditures combined add up to $60 billion—more than 30 percent of the total amount spent annually on health care.

According to John Knowles, former president of the Rockefeller Foundation and editor of the book, *Doing Better and Feeling Worse* (W.W. Norton and Company, 1979), 99 percent of us are born healthy and made sick by personal behavior and/or environmental conditions. Aaron Wildavsky, former head of the Russell Sage Foundation, claims that 90 percent of all illness is caused by factors beyond the doctor's control—eating habits, smoking, the lack of exercise, and unhealthful conditions in the environment and the workplace.

Studies conducted by Dr. Lester Breslow and Associates in southern California indicate a direct correlation between continued good health and seven simple practices: (1) getting seven to eight hours of sleep each night; (2) eating breakfast regularly; (3) staying slightly below one's normal weight; (4) avoiding between-meal snacks; (5) taking planned exercise—sports, walking, or vigorous work; (6) using alcohol moderately or not at all; and (7) refraining from smoking.

The more of these seven practices one adopts, the longer one stays healthy. For example, a 45-year-old man who follows three of them faithfully can expect to live to the age of 67, while following six or seven extends that to 78— a gain of 11 years. In other words, it really *is* within each person's power to add to his or her own life expectancy by exchanging unhealthy habits for healthy ones.

Living and working environments also affect one's health. Dr. Roy Menninger, president of the Menninger Foundation, estimates that 80 percent of the complaints people commonly take to their doctors—including colds, upset stomachs, back pains, the loss of appetite, insomnia, and fatigue—are not physical ills as much as they are psychosomatic reactions to the problems of daily life. Moreover, Dr. Menninger asserts, emotional tensions and anxieties contribute directly to the growing incidence of serious illness. As people experience stress and strain, they often respond by smoking, eating poorly, abusing alcohol or drugs, or failing to exercise regularly.

America's unparalleled standard of living has resulted in some lamentable by-products: sedentariness, the overconsumption of food and chemicals, and the inability to cope with an increasingly complex world. We have conquered such dreaded diseases as smallpox and polio; we have yet to confront the diseases stemming from the fact that our country is a far less healthy place to live and work than it used to be.

Rising health care costs have triggered an increase in

public awareness and a demand for solutions. Unfortunately, however, many of the attempts at solutions—such as national health insurance, the regulated distribution of health care, and mounting government controls—have only served to aggravate the situation.

The answer lies in adopting a totally new attitude toward health. As a nation, we must learn to accept the idea that individuals and communities are responsible for their own well-being. We must also change our thinking to perceive good health as a natural condition, and illness and injury as departures from the norm. We must stop defining health as the absence of disease. These points have been stressed by the World Health Organization, the 1970 and 1977 Conferences on Future Directions in Health Care, the World Council of Churches, and the National Council of Churches.

Slowly but surely, the promotion of good health is becoming a major social movement. It is gaining in popularity for a number of reasons: rising health care costs; the fact that people's health is not improving in proportion to the dollars being spent for medical and hospital care; and a growing understanding that lifestyles and personal habits are responsible for much of the unnecessary sickness and disability Americans experience. Finally, people are beginning to realize that medical care following the onset of illness has its limitations.

As it now stands, our health care system is illness-oriented. Health care providers have a tradition of not giving consumers access to information that will help them to help themselves. Organized medicine will no doubt continue to provide excellent care for episodic illnesses, and will no doubt broaden its focus somewhat to incorporate more health promotion, but whether it will make a significant contribution to upgrading the nation's health and wellness is open to question. Simply stated, the system operates under too many constraints. It is not likely that it will be able to heal itself.

While the government's efforts in the area of the national health have been extensive, they have not been particularly effective. Massive expenditures for medical research and health care delivery have not measurably improved the health of very many people. Even the most promising projects—like the U.S. Navy's program on alcohol abuse—have not been widely implemented. And most government policies on health, including recent ones aimed at containing costs, have only driven costs upward.

Thus, we cannot turn to either the health care system or to the government for solutions. We can, however, turn to business.

Up until now, business involvement in health care has consisted primarily of paying the bills. Corporations devote hundreds of millions of dollars annually to employee health benefit plans, and smaller companies earmark equally significant amounts of their resources for this purpose. What most businesses do, in other words, is to support the system as it exists. At Control Data, we feel that the role of business should be to *improve* the system and, where necessary, *change* it.

In 1974, we acquired a claims-processing company called Systems Resources, now Control Data Benefit Services. In 1977, we established a Healthcare Services group for the purpose of coordinating a number of health-related programs and services in which we were becoming involved. In 1980, we began using Control Data Benefit Services to handle all internal health claims. The system employs advanced computer technology to interpret complex benefit programs and ensure the accuracy of payments made. Over the past two years, we have been able to contain our health claim costs and measurably improve the management of our employee benefit programs. Recently, we have begun marketing the system to other companies.

In 1975, we acquired the Medlab Company, a Salt Lake City-based developer of clinical computer systems. Its principal product is PATHLAB, an information and management system for clinical laboratories. In 1978, we acquired the Life Extension Institute (LEI), a leading nationwide organization which offers a wide range of preventive medicine and health maintenance programs to business, including physical examinations, medical management services, and occupational and worksite health programs.

As we worked with the physicians, behavorial psychologists, and health educators at the LEI, we began wondering whether it would be possible to deliver effective health services at our company worksites. The idea seemed like one whose time had come. It is not uncommon for Control Data to employ two or more members of the same family; our work force is stable for the most part; and experience has shown that employees are far more willing to participate in health programs offered at work than those offered elsewhere.

We knew that many major U.S. corporations had already tried different approaches to health care, ranging from on-site physical examinations to a variety of programs devoted to exercise, fitness, blood pressure control, weight control, self-assessment, health data collection, alcohol counseling, and smoking cessation. We also knew that most such programs had achieved only marginal success. A corporate medical director, or a jobber, or perhaps a benefits manager or an unusually well-informed chief executive might take part, but the effects usually did not extend to the general employee population.

After careful consideration and planning, we decided to implement a corporate-wide health program of our own. Inaugurated in 1979, StayWell has the workplace as its focal point. It operates on the principle of personal responsibility, and is designed to promote good health through lifestyle change. Although its primary emphasis is on physical health, there are obvious areas of overlap between physical and mental well-being, and in many ways it addresses both.

The program begins with a confidential, computer-aided assessment of each participant's current state of health and future prospects. The information garnered from that assessment is used to compile a profile that illustrates the relationship between the person's chronological age and what we term his or her "health risk age." The profile then guides participants in setting lifestyle-change goals, the underlying premise being that individuals can learn to alter behaviors that are harmful to their health.

During the next phase, participants are given training in the skills they need to change negative habits. Courses on topics ranging from weight control, physical fitness, and nutrition to stress control and smoking cessation are delivered on site during free-time hours. Post-course support groups are formed to help participants continue their lifestyle change efforts, and employee task forces are organized for interested employees who wish to make their work environments healthier. Thus far, task forces have been responsible for the development of salad bars and more nutritious menus in company dining facilities, jogging courses on company property, worksite no-smoking areas, and permanent fitness programs.

To date, over 17,000 Control Data employees and many of their spouses have participated in StayWell. The program will eventually be made available to our entire U.S. work force of approximately 50,000.

Annual health-risk appraisals and physical screenings will enable participants to assess their health status on a continuing basis and explore possibilities for improvement. An elaborate computer-based evaluation program will measure the effects of StayWell on the total employee population over an extended period of time, taking into account such factors as productivity, absenteeism, and the use of employee health benefits.

StayWell is a holistic health program that we expect will yield significant results over the long term. It is unique in that it is based on personal commitment, goal setting, and behavior change—approaches to health that require new types of learning and new attitudes on the part of the learner. PLATO, our computer-based education and training system, will be the primary teaching tool for StayWell. It will enable us to deliver, reliably and economically, the massive amounts of multi-media training that will be required—an undertaking that would not be possible without computer technology. We believe that PLATO will prove to be the only effective and practicable means of disseminating health education and information to a wide audience while simultaneously responding to individual user needs, and we are devoting substantial time and effort to generating applicable courseware.

Developed initially for internal use, StayWell is now being marketed to other corporations. But we want to do more than sell the program; we want to cooperate with other corporations to ensure its use by large numbers of people. We believe in the program, and we believe that techniques for individualized self-health management must be disseminated widely and rapidly, not just for the sake of our own employees, but also because society stands to benefit greatly from this undertaking.

Plans are currently being made to modify StayWell so that it can be applied in impoverished rural and urban areas, both of which have a pressing need for better, more affordable, and more readily accessible health care. In this regard, we are looking to the federal government and to other corporations to provide major financial support and to assist us in creating a new kind of public-private partnership.

There is much to be gained from this type of effort. Our society's resources would be used more efficiently. New kinds of profitable business opportunities would open up for the private sector. Health care providers would begin to play a more appropriate role. We would all become less dependent on government for decisions that affect our health—and, most importantly, we would realize a higher level of physical and mental well-being.

Of course, there will be many obstacles to face and risks to take in the years ahead. But anybody who grasps the seriousness of our current health care problems—and foresees the adverse consequences of continuing to ignore them—will view these obstacles and risks as acceptable.

In the not-so-distant past, most health care was provided in the home and depended largely on family-based efforts. In recent decades, the trend has been to move nearly all essential health services out of the home and into doctors' offices and highly specialized medical complexes. While this has proved beneficial in some ways, it is hardly cost-effective, and it has engendered a kind of medical dependency that has made us less healthy as a society.

It is time to decentralize the health system once again, to shift the responsibility for health back to the workplace and the home and from there to the individual and his or her family. In short, it is time to revolutionize health care in America. Only by so doing will we enable all people, no matter who they are or where they live, to manage their own lives more effectively and more healthfully.

PART THREE

9

Worker Performance and Productivity

Lagging productivity growth in the United States has been a cause of great concern during recent years. Our economy is faltering, and we no longer enjoy our previously strong competitive position in the international marketplace. The American worker is still the most productive in the world, but by a rapidly decreasing margin. Twenty years ago, for example, the average French or German worker was half as productive as the typical American worker, and the Japanese worker one-fourth as productive; by 1979, French and German productivity had risen to four-fifths of that of the United States, and Japan's had climbed to two-thirds of our level. Thus, while we have retained our leadership status, we are now facing the very real challenge of keeping others from passing us by.

A number of explanations have been posited for our failure to maintain a higher productivity rate. Some critics point to the fact that American workers seem to have lost much of their pride in workmanship. Others argue that the post-World War II influx into the labor market of inexperienced workers—notably women and minorities—has slowed us down. Still others claim that our system of taxation is at fault, and that high marginal rates on personal incomes, taxes on savings, and inadequate depreciation allowances have combined to discourage the volume of savings and capital investments needed to expand productivity.

Obviously, a large share of the blame can be placed on inflation, which has added to investment uncertainty and contributed to the high interest rates that retard investments. In addition, businesses have been forced to ex-

SOURCE

"Technology for Company-Employee Partnership To Improve Productivity" address, Direction '81 Conference, Minneapolis, Minnesota, December 2, 1980. (Also presented to the American Institute of Industrial Engineers, Minneapolis, Minnesota, December 8, 1980.)

pend an inordinate amount of time and effort on satisfying government regulations. Finally, it has been said that the educational establishment—particularly the business schools—have exacerbated the situation by continuing to place undue emphasis on short-term gains, causing a decline in long-term research and product and technical development.

All of these factors have undoubtedly contributed to our current dilemma. In my judgment, however, the tendency for costs to rise at a faster rate than productivity is primarily the result of the under utilization of our human resources. I am also convinced that finding solutions to our problems is more the responsibility of management than of labor, and that the eventual outcome will depend strongly on the extent to which employers are willing to assist employees in achieving greater productivity.

At Control Data, we are dedicated to the development of a corporate culture that stresses the more effective utilization of human resources. The nature of our business makes this imperative. We are at the forefront of the trend that is changing the United States from an industrial society to an information society; only about 20 percent of all American workers today are engaged in manufacturing. Our continued success depends heavily on our employees' attitudes and behaviors. We feel that we must expend more effort than ever before in responding to the personal needs of our workers in equitable, responsible, humanitarian ways.

In keeping with this philosophy, we have embarked on a multifaceted and highly creative program called "Fair Exchange: A Partnership for Excellence." It is a partnership, a shared commitment, in every sense of the word. We help our employees to attain their personal and career goals; they in turn agree to help us to attain our corporate objectives.

Fair Exchange is based on two premises: (1) that any organization's effectiveness is essentially a function of its human resources; and (2) that people perform best in a caring and supportive environment. The keystone of the program is innovation. This is evident in the numerous "enabling technologies" we have created for our employees to enrich their professional and personal lives and in our expectations of the people who work for us.

First and foremost among the enabling technologies available to our workers is PLATO, our computer-based education and training system. Through PLATO, we offer a broad range of courses directed at improving the job skills and human relations skills of both management and non-management personnel.

A serious problem exists within our society at the present time. Our schools are not providing students with the knowledge they need in order to survive and function in the working world. In the past, each new generation has achieved a higher level of learning than the preceding one; today, young people come out of high school less skilled than their parents were. Too many graduates lack the basic skills necessary to get a first job or to fully master further vocational or professional training.

We believe that substandard performance goes hand-in-hand with inadequate training and education, and that not having the skills to do a job right leads to despair, that despair leads to apathy, and that apathy engenders shoddy workmanship. We envision PLATO as the technology that will bridge the gap between people's skills and the requirements of the job market.

We place special emphasis on developing our managers' human relations abilities. Most managers are adept at getting things done, but they tend to be far better at controlling and directing non-human factors such as assets, design efforts, and production methods than at managing human beings. They find it difficult to adapt to matrix management, an approach which requires them to play several roles—boss, peer, and follower—often within the course of a single afternoon. In short, they need help in the form of training. PLATO is providing this training through its extensive array of course offerings. Non-management personnel are offered functional training in all categories including purchasing, personnel, accounting, marketing, and clerical.

Under their commitment to Fair Exchange, our employees recognize that they are expected to devote whatever time and effort it takes to acquire the job skills they need and keep improving on them. Through our appraisal system, they are made aware of courses available to them and steered toward those that will benefit them the most. Each employee meets at least once a year with a manager or supervisor to discuss performance expectations and individual development, and to formulate mutually agreeable plans for further growth. While taking courses is not a requirement for continued employment, it is generally understood that the degree of an employee's participation in the training effort and his or her resulting level of achievement are considered when it comes time to determine promotions and pay increases.

PLATO represents a substantial portion of our investment in Fair Exchange. Since we began offering courses through it in 1975, the system has aptly demonstrated its versatility and its capacity to deliver accessible, affordable, high-quality education and training. In 1981, Control Data employees took nearly 300,000 hours of formal course work through PLATO. These included a high proportion of our non-management personnel, as well as the more than 5,000 managers who averaged nearly 46 hours each of training designed to upgrade their technical, conceptual, and human relations skills. Several hundred newly hired managers completed 50-hour training programs within 90 days of commencing employment.

Among the sequences required of managers is a series of three courses in Principles of Affirmative Action and Minority Group Awareness. Largely as a result of this training program, Control Data has acquired an enviable affirmative action record, with minority employees constituting approximately 15 percent of out total work force.

Three additional PLATO courses deserve mention here: Concerned Others, Helping Relationship, and Parenting. Concerned Others is aimed at helping persons whose families are experiencing alcohol and other drug-related problems. It presents the facts and signs of alcohol and drug abuse, and tells people how and where to get assistance. Helping Relationship teaches communications and helping skills via courseware and peer counseling. Based on the belief that little problems left untended can become bigger and more serious, it has been extremely effective for employees who are facing minor personal difficulties and emotional setbacks. Finally, Parenting is a skills-oriented resource parents can use to learn how to deal with the uncertainty and fear often associated with the task of child-rearing.

We are gearing up for what may amount to as much as a tenfold increase over traditional levels of employee training, and our primary vehicle will remain PLATO CBE. We are greatly encouraged by the fact that operating costs have decreased dramatically over the years. In 1975, costs averaged about $7 per hour; today they are close to $2 per hour. In contrast, other training methods average $18 to $75 per hour.

Two specific examples will serve to demonstrate the economic benefits of utilizing PLATO. By replacing 25 days of classroom training with 19 days of PLATO training for new computer programmer analysts, we have saved approximately $5,000 per student while simultaneously providing a higher-grade course content. And by using PLATO to teach employees how to maintain customer equipment, we have realized a training cost reduction of around $700,000 per year.

There are other less tangible benefits that have accrued from the company-wide implementation of PLATO CBE. Many employees have access to PLATO terminals at their work sites, and they can take courses at times convenient to them; as a result, more employees participate in the training effort than would otherwise be the case. We make it relatively easy for workers to take PLATO courses, and they report that the frequent brief periods of training during the work day stimulate them while simultaneously upgrading their skills.

PLATO is also central to a number of special programs developed for Control Data employees, most notably Homework, Work-At-Home, and StayWell. The Homework program is a training and development alternative for the severely disabled homebound population. Currently, participants are engaged in programming computers, preparing data, and designing educational courseware. Homework also serves as a means of communication among participants, who learn different skills at different rates while sharing the learning experience. They are assisted by a counselor assigned to the program.

Work-At-Home uses PLATO to allow a growing number of able-bodied employees to work in their homes for two, three, or four days a week. StayWell delivers health education with emphasis on individual lifestyle changes.

Another important enabling technology not connected with PLATO is EAR, our Employee Advisory Resource program. EAR was established in 1974 to assist employees, their spouses, and their dependents with family, financial, legal, chemical, personal, and work-related problems. By dialing a toll-free number from anywhere in the country, an individual can contact one of 26 full- and part-time counselors who are available 24 hours a day. The counselor listens, helps to diagnose the problem, and offers possible solutions on a strictly confidential basis. The caller is assured completely anonymity.

Each EAR counselor is trained in crisis-intervention techniques and is knowledgeable about local community services that the caller can turn to for help or treatment. In the event of a work-related problem, the counselor works with the caller and his or her manager—with the caller's permission—to seek and interpret relevant facts and arrive at a just solution.

Since its inception, more than 40,000 members of Control Data's labor force have turned to EAR, and new calls are coming in at a rate of over 700 per month. On the average, 45 percent of the calls address work-related problems and 55 percent are of a personal nature.

In terms of reduced labor turnover, absenteeism, and medical costs, we estimate that EAR saves Control Data about $10 million annually. These savings, while substantial, are dwarfed by the immeasurable but very real benefits that the program has provided to our employees. Consistent with our policy of turning social needs into profitable business opportunities, we are now marketing EAR to other corporations under the name of Employee Assistance Program, or EAP.

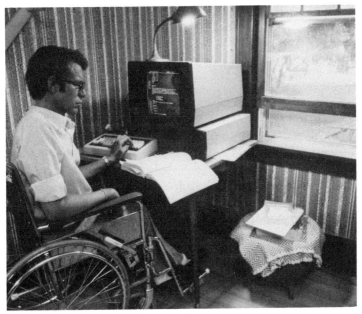

PLATO is central to a number of special programs...most notably HOMEWORK, Work-at-Home, and Staywell.... The Selby plant (below) employs part-time workers...the morning shift is made up of mothers with school-age children.

In these days of persistent inflation, people everywhere are finding it harder to stretch their paychecks, and our employees are no exception. Our WiserWays program helps them to counter the devastating effects of inflation by showing them how to make better use of their personal incomes. WiserWays offers a wide spectrum of services, including PLATO courses on creating a tax-oriented budget, money management, the proper use of credit, investment and insurance planning, and comparison shopping; a Ride Sharing program, a FactFile containing valuable money-saving tips that is given free of charge to employees who request it; and volume discounts on merchandise and food. By calling our Employee Information Center, workers can find out about WiserWays and other Control Data programs and services directed toward inflation fighting.

As part of our commitment to creating a new business culture within Control Data, we have made significant changes in our employee benefits and protections programs over the years. For example, we provide all full-time employees and their spouses with extensive health and dental insurance in addition to the more traditional life, disability, and dismemberment coverage. Under our employee retirement plan, participants are entitled to a vested interest in their accrued benefits after ten years and to full benefits at age 65. Our Social Service Leave policy, introduced in 1977, allows employees to continue receiving their normal company salaries while working for non-profit organizations on social problems. Most leaves are short-term, but a limited number of long-term leaves are granted, some extending up to a year.

Employee grievances are processed through a series of reviews by successively higher levels of management. In 1974, this system of employee justice was enhanced by the addition of an ombudsman specifically charged with ensuring that the review process works for the employees as well as for the company. In the planning stages is a ''court-of-last-resort,'' where workers will be able to go for peer group review or arbitration. We feel that this will not only enhance our reputation for fairness among our employees, but also result in substantial savings for us due to fewer lawsuits and an improved company position in the event of those that are filed. It should be noted that we carefully safeguard the privacy of employee information and records while simultaneously guaranteeing employee access to such materials.

Job security is uppermost in most employees' minds in an era when plant closings are becoming commonplace, and we are doing our best to provide our workers with a sense that their employment with us is protected. Normally, a large company responds to a severe turndown by reducing inventories, laying off workers, and closing selected plants; we consider these responses neither equitable nor acceptable. Thus, we have been working toward establishing a policy on the maintenance of employment. We are re-evaluating such issues as the extent to which employment levels should be maintained beyond those required for maximum credit efficiency; we are also examining alternatives to plant closings, ranging from spreading workloads among several plants to offering employees the option of taking unpaid vacations in times of adversity. Most importantly, we are continuing our long-term effort to create sources of new jobs.

In general, our basic strategy has always been to look beyond the customary and legal requirements of employees' benefits and rights. Instead of merely reacting to disputes or complaints, we have tried to anticipate how and when such situations or concerns might manifest themselves. We have then proceeded proactively to develop programs that balance workers' individual rights with the company's responsibilities and obligations.

We value our employees' input and suggestions when developing new programs or modifying existing ones. Each year, we randomly select some ten percent of our work force to participate in attitude surveys. We ask them to tell us how they feel about their jobs and working conditions, and how they view the overall management and direction of the company. These annual surveys are a tangible demonstration of our concern for our employees, and play a key role in our employee relations effort.

We also encourage employees to participate in company involvement teams, small groups which meet voluntarily on a regular basis to identify and analyze work-related problems, recommend solutions, and, where possible, implement the solutions themselves. The Involvement team members not only consider production problems, but also focus on those relating to morale, working conditions, communications, and organizational effectiveness. The results have been encouraging and clearly demonstrate the extent to which Control Data workers are concerned and willing, when given the chance, to apply their knowledge and expertise to improving the work environment.

Over the years, we have taken a number of steps to make Control Data a desirable and accommodating employer. For example, we have developed several alternatives to the traditional nine-to-five, in-the-office work week. We realize that many individuals are eager to work, but are unable for whatever reason to be at the work site during regular office hours. Mention has already been made of the Homework and Work-At-Home programs which allow employees with special needs to work in their homes. Related innovations include the establishment of separate shifts for groups of employees at our inner-city Selby plant in St. Paul, Minnesota; the location of satellite offices in areas with a high concentration of employee residences; and the introduction of a company-wide flexible hours program.

The Selby plant employs three groups of part-time workers. The morning shift is made up of mothers with school-age children, and the afternoon and evening shifts consist of students working their way through school or supplementing their families' incomes. Since 1970, the Selby plant has consistently provided work opportunities for a force of approximately 280 employees who might not otherwise have found suitable jobs.

The option of working either in satellite offices or in their homes has served to increase employees' productivity by reducing the time and energy needed to get to and from work and relieving the stresses inherent in commuting long distances over congested highways. Those workers not attracted by a regular office routine have the added advantage of being able to set their own work schedules, within reasonable limits.

In 1972, we radically modified our company's work patterns by instituting a flexible hours program. Participating individuals or groups are permitted to vary their work schedules as long as they satisfy two requirements: they must not alter the number of hours they work each day, and the work flow must not be disturbed. The program has been in operation for more than a decade, and it is considered one of the major benefits of working for Control Data, with some 65 percent of our domestic labor force currently making use of it. It has been found to substantially alleviate the frustrations and pressures involved in getting to and from work during rush hour, resulting in an accompanying decline in tardiness and the use of sick leaves as well as a significant upsurge in productivity.

In light of the various programs and benefits we offer our workers, it should come as no surprise that we expect each employee to make a long-term commitment to Control Data. Yet it is not our intent to categorically equate the interests of an individual with those of a large company. When it becomes evident that a mismatch has occurred in spite of everyone's best efforts, it is sometimes preferable for an employee to resign. Yet we view the resignation decision as a positive event and leave the door open should he or she decide to rejoin us later. Some of our most valued employees are those who have left us and then returned.

We will even provide employees who wish to leave with reasonable assistance in making the change. For example, should an employee wish to start a small company, we will consult with him or her in formulating a business plan. On the average, about 15 employees per month seek this type of assistance, and one in ten actually decides to try starting a business of his or her own. The remainder discover somewhere along the way that it's not for them and opt to remain with us.

Fair Exchange has already been defined as a partnership; it could just as well be described as a mutual support system. In an age when a growing segment of American society is becoming increasingly mobile, the pressures on the family are escalating. Either by choice or because of frequent transfers, families are leaving behind many of their traditional support systems—relatives, childhood friends, neighborhoods, churches, and so on. As a consequence, they often have nowhere to turn in times of stress. It is incumbent upon employers to provide their employees with a spectrum of support services, both direct and indirect. At Control Data, direct support services include EAR, WiserWays, alternative work programs, PLATO training courses, and innovative benefits and protections; indirect support services are left up to individual facilities and range all the way from employee gardens to recreational programs.

It would be naive to assume that people come to work for us simply because they are attracted by EAR and the chance to participate in company baseball teams. The major motivators are the opportunities to do a job, do it well, and be rewarded through merit pay increases and promotions—all within a caring environment. Our employees appreciate our willingness to train them, help them to advance, and encourage them to stay with us. Our efforts to provide our workers with rewarding lives are matched by their conscientious response.

It should be stressed that we do not offer built-in special recognition programs, and that an employee's long-term success does not depend on them. We recognize that the values people place on their work vary widely. Job security is of utmost importance to some; money is paramount to others; and there are those who equate their careers with their social status. Given these and other differences, it is not practical to design an effective company-wide method of recognition. This does not preclude the possibility that special programs will be offered from time to time; in fact, it is assumed that they will be offered on appropriate occasions, such as when a severe competitive problem exists or the quality of a product is questioned.

Thus far, we have been very pleased by the extent to which both our employees and the company as a whole have achieved their respective goals under the Fair Exchange program. In 1982, an Employee Attitude Survey showed that over 80 percent of the 4,100 workers contacted were satisfied with and dedicated to their jobs. Our labor turnover and absentee rates are well below those of most other companies. Of the employees who have left

Control Data at one time or another, some 5,000—nearly 8.5 percent of our total labor force—have eventually come back.

The bottom line is, of course, productivity. Over the past five years, Control Data's productivity level per worker has grown at an impressive annual rate of close to 3.4 percent. And surveys have revealed that our employees consider themselves less productive than they are capable of being or desire to be. They keep wanting to try harder!

The statistics are gratifying, but we are not content to rest upon them. We recognize that we must continue to develop new programs and implement new policies if we are to realize more fully the productive potential of our labor force. At the same time, we are convinced that our experience has demonstrated how American industry can more effectively respond to the productivity challenge by making better use of its human resources.

No discussion of productivity growth would be complete without some reference to Japan's impressive performance. Most of that country's success has been attributed to the behaviors and attitudes of its work force, which are rooted in Japanese culture. Briefly, the Japanese have a stronger sense of community and a weaker sense of the self than Americans do. This cultural difference is especially evident in the work place. American workers regularly and hotly compete with one another; competition between Japanese workers is virtually nonexistent. Instead, the Japanese compete on the company level, and employees of individual companies perceive themselves as working in concert toward a common goal: producing quality products in a timely and efficient way.

Japan's seniority system forms the basis of this approach. Japanese workers receive pay increases primarily because of seniority and not because of exceptional individual contributions. In addition, the option of "lifetime employment," while not available to all workers, has a perceptible effect on employee performance. A worker whose future rests with the company will behave in ways that will benefit the company the most; it is taken for granted that if the company thrives, so will the employee.

The larger Japanese companies also provide their employees with a wider variety of services than their American counterparts, including subsidized housing, transportation, health care, child care, and educational and recreational programs. Management practices are more participatory than in the United States. Ironically, the involvement team concept mentioned earlier stems from American concepts of participative management; the Japanese have simply taken the idea further, improved on it, and popularized it.

Whenever Japan is set forth as an example of productivity, there is the temptation to jump on the bandwagon and insist that their way is the best way. It may indeed be best for Japan—the evidence in support of it is certainly there—but it is not the way American business can or should go. The Japanese work attitude, and the paternalism exercised by Japan's large companies, cannot be transferred intact to America; the cultural disparities are too great. We can, however, adopt certain of their practices to our benefit. Specifically, we can place more emphasis on employee education and training; we can instill an atmosphere of cooperation within industry and between industry and government; and we can take a longer-term view rather than continually stressing short-term gains and objectives.

Japanese companies view the investment in employee education and training as a worthwhile and relatively low-risk one. If an employee is going to be around for years to come, it makes sense to devote considerable resources to training and retraining him or her. Although Americans might not be ready to accept the idea of lifetime employment, this does not mean that we should not vastly step up employee education and training. With computer-based systems such as PLATO, we can now do this effectively and efficiently. We can protect our investment by surrounding our employees with a caring and responsive work environment—one in which they will want to stay.

A distinguishing feature of the Japanese system—or Japan, Inc., as it is often called—is the evident cooperation within industry and between industry and government. Americans are accustomed to drawing a heavy line between the private and public sectors; in Japan, the government plays an active and welcome role in industrial development. It provides planning guidance to several selected industries, awards subsidies for R&D, and encourages companies to pool their resources and innovations. American companies, in contrast, are more concerned with protecting their proprietary interests and guarding their own turf, and the relationship between industry and government is a traditionally adversarial one. This must change, and it must change quickly, if we are to compete with the Japanese; industrial innovation is too pivotal to be kept secret. Even the most highly motivated and skilled work force will not be able to hold its own in the world marketplace unless the innovations embodied in capital, equipment, processes and methods, the creation of new products and services, and the improvement of existing products and services are shared.

The results of Japanese cooperation are nowhere more evident than on America's highways, which are teeming with Japanese automobiles. American cars can no longer compete. Part of this is due to the fact that Japan took the long view of the world energy situation; they saw the crisis coming when we did not, and we made bad decisions.

Japanese productivity is and will continue to be a force to be reckoned with. Rather than letting it intimidate us, though, we should concentrate on regaining our own former competitive position. We have the resources and the know-how to do it, but the outcome will depend on how well we establish and implement a new corporate culture within our borders. This new corporate culture must rest firmly on expanded innovation, expanded investments in human resources, greater cooperation, and a strong emphasis on caring.

The innovations we must strive for are those which will provide the products and services that will meet our society's major unmet needs. Investments in human resources must include vast increases in employee education and training which stresses the value of consistently high levels of performance and productivity. Cooperation must begin within industries and extend to encompass industry and government, with the government taking the responsibility for maintaining and stimulating employment. Caring must include the use of company resources to help employees help themselves in solving the problems of everyday living.

Every American company must make a firm commitment to doing what it can to improve its employees' lives. Every employee must make an equally firm commitment to achieving and sustaining a high level of conscientious performance. If we share in the effort, utilize the resources we have at our disposal, and move ahead intelligently, we will make lagging productivity growth a thing of the past.

10

Mergers, Acquisitions, and Plant Closings

Whenever an executive addresses the topic of mergers—especially forced takeovers—it is immediately assumed that he fears for his own company's survival. Let me emphasize that my interest in the subject does not stem from any unspoken apprehension that Control Data will be the target of a hostile takeover attempt either now or in the future. The nature of our business safeguards us to some extent; other large companies that are not familiar with the computer field do not know how to succeed in it, and, as has been aptly demonstrated in recent years, they would be foolish to try. General Electric and RCA lost hundreds of millions of dollars when they undertook the management of computer businesses, and this has effectively discouraged other noncomputer companies from mounting takeover efforts against companies like Control Data. As far as other large computer companies are concerned, we are effectively shielded from unwelcome advances on their part by antitrust legislation. Finally, we have put into place a number of corporate policies that further protect our employees, our stockholders, and other stakeholders from injury in the unlikely possibility that someone might attempt a hostile merger.

I should also make it clear that I am not categorically opposed to all corporate mergers. Some mergers can be mutually beneficial, especially those involving small companies with complementary products or services, or companies that are having financial difficulties, or companies that are unable to cope sufficiently with a severe competitive disadvantage because they lack adequate resources. Under these and related circumstances, it may be impossi-

SOURCES

"Irresponsible Mergers and Acquisitions" address, Corporate Development Institute Seminar, New York, New York, March 4, 1980.

"Constructive Plant Closing Legislation" address, Directors Conference, Hilton Head, South Carolina, October 8, 1980.

ble for a company to preserve its assets or avoid cutting back on its employment without at least considering a merger. There are other examples of meritorious mergers; because of differences among industries and among companies within individual industries, each must be evaluated on its own terms.

I am chiefly concerned with power-play corporate takeovers, those in which one company is captured by another simply because the acquiring company covets the target company and has the financial means to go after it. In these instances, little or no regard is given to the impact the merger will have on the target company's employees, on its customers, or on society in general. I strongly believe that unwelcome mergers are a plague on the national community; evidence to support this view is found in the economic and social trauma that a hostile merger invariably leaves in its wake.

The attempted takeover of Gerber Products Company by Anderson, Clayton & Co. in 1977 vividly illustrates the human trauma unwelcome takeover efforts are likely to involve, even when they ultimately prove unsuccessful. The case attracted national press attention. On July 27 of that year, *The Wall Street Journal* observed that "...one concern is that if it wins control of Gerber, Anderson, Clayton might cut back on Gerber's 125-person research operation [in Gerber's Fremont, Michigan, home community] or on other white collar staffs, consolidating them with its similar departments elsewhere." On October 2, *The New York Times* reported: "The takeover campaign created unrest in Fremont, though Anderson, Clayton insisted throughout that it had no intention of moving jobs from Fremont." The *Times* article went on to quote Fremont's mayor as saying, "I think you are seeing a panic situation in town right now. Everybody is concerned because they don't know what the future will bring." When it became clear that the takeover attempt had failed, the Fremont newspaper ran this headline: "Gerber Employees Get Over Merger-Itis Fear."

Generally speaking, a desirable or necessary merger is most likely to be a friendly one. A contested takeover, on the other hand, will be publicly opposed by the target company's board, indicating that the proposed merger does not make business and economic sense to them. Moreover, in the case of a hotly contested merger, it is virtually impossible to do the advance planning necessary to minimize the impact of adverse aftereffects.

Even when a merger is welcome and carefully planned, some unavoidable injuries to employee careers will result, along with other injustices arising from the process of forcing two organizations together. This is especially true when one of the parties is a large company. Senior executives of the acquired company find that their positions have been eliminated by the takeover. Younger executives aspiring to membership in the top management body discover that their career paths have been blocked. It is understandable that there will be profound differences between the duties and responsibilities and rewards of the parent company's top-level executives and those of the subsidiary company's management, but this does not make the circumstances any less painful.

Job jeopardy is foremost in the minds of employees at other levels as well. When administrative and operational functions are consolidated, jobs are frequently eliminated outright. Many workers have strong community ties, and cutbacks and/or plant closings often present them with two equally unattractive options: going on unemployment, or trying to find jobs in other parts of the country and leaving their support systems behind. In a voluntary merger, the consolidating process can be better managed to minimize these social injustices.

The issue is further complicated by the fact that companies make commitments to their employees, both implied and stated, relating to job responsibilities and career paths. Employees expect these commitments to be honored while simultaneously understanding that competition, adverse economic conditions, and other factors not under the complete control of management may result in some of them not being met. There is generally an atmosphere of give-and-take rooted in a sense of mutual trust. But when another company comes in and performs an unnecessary and unilateral takeover, this trust is violated. Commitments are cold-bloodedly and unjustly left by the wayside

—cold-bloodedly in that the aggressor company knows the consequences of breaking such commitments, and unjustly in that it is often possible to preserve many if not all of them by achieving the takeover objectives in another, more thoughtful way.

The most serious and least understood consequence of an unwarranted merger is the destruction of job-creating resources. Technological innovation is the wellspring of new jobs, the majority of which originate in the entrepreneurial environment of small enterprises. A small business typically begins by developing ideas and inventions into useful products and services, and this becomes a way of life that allows it to hold its own in competition with the giants.

Immediately following a forced takeover, the larger acquiring organization blankets the other with its bureaucracy. The smaller company is suddenly confronted with layer upon layer of parent company management, which is often more adept at blocking than making decisions. An innovation-stifling process sets in. Faced with the rising costs of R&D, the risks involved in launching new products, and relentless pressure from its own stockholders to increase short-term earnings, the larger company opts to improve existing products and reduce labor content and materials costs. Ideas for novel products or services are set aside or shelved. Even if a new product or service is finally approved, it must then run the gauntlet of those—and they are in the majority—who belittle the chances of success of any new undertaking. Finally, the project must survive the foot-dragging, road-blocking administrative procedures that invariably follow.

This innovation-stifling process is compounded by the fact that the more creative employees of the acquired company are normally the first to resign. The original entrepreneurial team—the major job-creating resource of the smaller company—is dispersed and ultimately lost. This is a prime example of the human and economic waste that is fueling inflation.

The parent company's stockholders are shielded from the adverse effects of an unwelcome merger, but society is not. When administrative and operating units are consolidated to increase productivity, this usually means the loss of jobs in an already shaky employment environment. The displaced workers must find employment elsewhere or go on unemployment compensation and perhaps eventually resort to welfare. In other words, the profits from the consolidation are achieved in part at society's expense.

The foregoing scenario of innovation stifling and the destruction of job-creating resources is not based on theory or second-hand information. Over the years, I have lived it many times—from both sides. I have worked for a company that was acquired by another, and I have overseen the acquisition of smaller companies by Control Data. Let me hasten to add that in the latter case the mergers have always been voluntary. Control Data has never participated in an unwelcome, unwarranted, or hostile takeover.

My experience as a member of an acquired organization began in 1952, when I was a senior executive of Engineering Research Associates (ERA), a highly innovative company that had been organized some six years earlier by a group of scientists and engineers. ERA had established a leadership position in the market for large-scale electronic computers, and its rapid growth had put it in a position of badly needing financing. The decision was made to sell ERA to the far larger Remington-Rand.

Within days after the takeover, Remington-Rand's bureaucracy had started to engulf ERA. A few of ERA's more impatient individuals immediately resigned. During the succeeding five years, most of ERA's remaining innovative employees followed, and in 1957 I left to organize Control Data.

No criticism of Remington-Rand or any other large corporation is implied here. It is simply that the bureaucracy in big organizations inevitably drives away creative personnel. This fact has been brought home to me several times since, when Control Data has been on the acquiring end of mergers.

The launching of Control Data represented the first publicly financed start-up in the computer industry. We were fully aware that our survival in a business already dominated by corporate giants required us to expand quickly. The acquisition of other small companies became an important part of the strategy we adopted to assemble the resources we needed. A number of these acquisitions turned out extremely well—some far beyond our expectations. This was due in part to our success in preserving a small-company atmosphere within Control Data, at least for a while. But the day came when we ourselves had become a big company. At that point, some of the most creative people we had added by means of various mergers began to leave, in spite of our best efforts to maintain an environment conducive to innovation.

A recent study of all acquisitions made by Control Data over a 22-year period showed that fewer than 15 percent of those employees who had been identified at the time of acquisition as members of the innovative team in each organization were still with us.

This record is hardly unique. According to a 1973 Hayes Associates study of 200 voluntary acquisitions made by a core group of Fortune 500 companies, only 42 percent of the top management personnel within the acquired companies stayed on for five years or longer. It can be assumed that the figures for all mergers would be significantly lower, since those companies who were willing to disclose their data tended to be ones that had compiled favorable records.

My experience with highly innovative small companies and bureaucratic giants alike has convinced me that a merger is not always the way to go. One company can often get the sought-for benefits of combining with another by means of licensing agreements, joint projects, or joint ownership. Any of these options can enable the larger company to achieve the legitimate objectives of a merger while preserving intact the innovative and job-creating resources of the other company and either eliminating or lessening the undesirable side effects.

There are many myths that stand in the way of creative alternatives to mergers. An especially popular one posits that the threat of a takeover provides a necessary check on inefficient management; in other words, the management of companies whose performance is substandard should come to expect takeover tenders if it fails to adequately improve performance. A 1979 study of mergers by Yale economist Dr. Merton Peck has effectively burst this theoretical bubble.

In examining mergers of mining and manufacturing companies with assets of $60 million or more, Peck found that the acquired firms were on balance far more profitable than the average firm within their industry. Harry Gray, chief executive officer of United Technologies, the leading company currently engaging in forced takeovers, has stated on numerous occasions that he uses three criteria when selecting target companies: profitability, market leadership, and proven management ability. He is not interested in poorly managed businesses.

The threat of a takeover is likely to have a negative effect on the management efficiency of even the most successful firms, because major policy decisions will often be made with primary consideration being given to the question of how they will affect the company's vulnerability. Several CEOs of medium-sized companies have told me personally that they have forgone undertaking the development of highly desirable products for fear that unforeseen problems would cause their companies' market price to fall, making them more susceptible to unwelcome merger attempts. It should be obvious that stockholders, employees, and constituent communities are all losers in this stifling milieu.

Another frequently advanced argument in favor of mergers is that they stimulate competition and economic efficiency. In truth, the synergistic results of corporate acquisitions are often overestimated at the outset. Nor does it appear that mergers—whether vertical, horizontal, mixed, or conglomerate—usually contribute significantly to the success of the companies involved. And mergers can be economically inefficient as far as society is concerned to the extent that they replace investments that might otherwise be made in new production and job-creating facilities.

At Control Data, we have established certain policies that pertain both to acquisitions we make and to the contingency of another company attempting to take us over. Basic to our policy on acquisitions is the understanding that business opportunities will be developed primarily from within. Exceptions are made, but only when it becomes clear that we cannot fill a need internally and can fill it by acquiring a company that wants to be acquired. Furthermore, in the event of an acquisition, we attempt whenever feasible to ensure that the objectives of both parties are achieved in a manner that leaves the innovating capabilities on all sides intact. For example, we might spin off a separate company, provide it with sufficient resources to support further innovation, and leave it under the control and management of the innovative team.

Our policy also requires that we conduct a social impact analysis during the earliest planning stages of a contemplated acquisition. Any projected adverse social impact that appears as though it could not reasonably be corrected is cause for rejection of the acquisition plan.

Briefly, each impact analysis includes a statement of our reasons for wanting to embark on the acquisition; five- and ten-year business plans detailing how the resulting business combination would be managed; and a thorough exploration of the anticipated effects that the acquisition would have on competition, productivity, workers' jobs and careers, suppliers, customers, stockholders, and constituent communities. Finally, we look closely at how the acquisition would impact the innovative capabilities of the acquired company.

We have taken two important steps to protect ourselves against the possibility of an unwelcome takeover. First, we have extended three-year employment security contracts to each member of our top management staff. Second, we have adopted a company-wide policy of social justice.

The employment security contracts, which are extended annually, would automatically be violated if reporting levels or job responsibilities were changed through a hostile takeover. Key personnel would be able to resign, collect more than two years' worth of their salaries, and seek employment elsewhere. It might appear that an aggressor company could buy off our executives with lucrative bonuses, but a strong consensus within Control Data that forced takeovers are akin to thuggery makes it unlikely that this approach would work, even if the other company were willing to pay the very large amounts of money required.

Our social justice policy makes it mandatory for Control Data's directors to consider all social factors, not price alone, when responding to a takeover offer. This policy was incorporated into our company charter in 1978 as an amendment; significantly, more than 95 percent of our individual stockholders voted in favor of it.

Finding solutions to the problems posed by unwelcome mergers should not rest solely on the shoulders of individual companies. A far better approach would be to enact legislation that would compel companies to judge the merits of proposed mergers on the basis of whether they would serve or harm society. Such an evaluation could entail a pre-merger social impact analysis similar to the one we use at Control Data. What I am suggesting is actually a more detailed version of the pre-merger notification procedure already required by the Federal Trade Commission, which tends to be one-dimensional in that it deals mainly with the effects that a merger would have on competition.

Who could be charged with judging the merits of a proposed merger? Either a government agency or the stockholders of the firms involved. I favor the latter, since I believe that stockholders can act responsibly if given the facts they need to make a decision and a structured procedure within which to work. If the legislation were to include a provision allowing any interested government agency, organization, or group, including employees, to file advocacy materials, the stockholders would be that much better informed.

I have broached this idea to many business leaders and financial analysts, and their response has been to question whether stockholders would actually look beyond the immediate financial considerations to the broader issues involved. This indicates to me that these business leaders and financial analysts have not had any relevant experience in dealing with stockholders and have not thought hard enough about what a government agency review would be like. Unless they have had occasion to seek approval of a merger decision, they have not learned first-hand that government agencies are typically afflicted with tunnel vision and are about as flexible as two-by-fours.

Although much is being written and said these days about corporate governance, very little of it is meaningful or practical. Requiring stockholders to vote on mergers would be a sensible and productive way to arrive at responsible corporate governance. In addition, the approach I am proposing would give employees a stronger voice in decisions affecting their jobs, an idea which has been advocated strongly over the past decade. And it would do so without impinging upon either the rights or the duties of management.

I am convinced that any legislation directed toward effectively eliminating forced takeovers would attract considerable support from corporate personnel. Most executives do not believe in hostile mergers and do not willingly engage in them. Yet they, too, are hired hands; loath to incur the displeasure of their directors or the investment community, and reluctant to intimate that they are vulnerable to takeovers, they do not speak out.

It is not fear alone that prevents them from taking a stand. Regrettably, many businessmen today do not comprehend how important innovation is to our economic well-being. They fail to see that innovation and potential sources of new jobs are stymied by a system that allows large firms to buy up highly innovative small- and medium-sized companies without first considering the ramifications of their actions. That system is sorely in need of reform.

The United States is unique in the world marketplace in that it allows private enterprise nearly unlimited freedom in the use of its resources. This freedom bears with it a high degree of accountability. Corporate resources must be used in creative and constructive ways that do not jeopardize or ignore the interests of society; to do otherwise is to invite the government to impose restrictions. Any unduly restrictive regulation on business activity today can almost unfailingly be traced back to business having assumed a reactionary or passive stance rather than taking the initiative to adapt to changing societal concerns.

The position of business in western Europe should serve

as a warning to us. In most western European countries, significant corporate mergers cannot be accomplished until the parties involved both obtain government approval and consult with workers' councils. Plant closings resulting in reduced employment are especially difficult and costly to achieve due to laws that require the participating companies to first obtain the approval of the workers and then compensate those who are laid off by paying their full salaries for up to two years.

In the United States, Maine and Wisconsin have already adopted laws governing plant closings, and New York and Minnesota are considering similar legislation. At the national level, a number of bills on the subject have been proposed to Congress. For example, the "Corporate Democracy Act of 1980" has been sponsored by a coalition called Americans Concerned About Corporate Power that comprises labor, consumer, environmental, and religious groups. Among its provisions is one requiring companies to give 24-month advance notice of plant relocations and shutdowns.

A plant closing is never a pleasant event. No one emerges unscathed: workers lose their jobs, community retailers lose business, the company incurs unemployment costs, and local government units must deal with the additional drain on their resources imposed by burgeoning unemployment and welfare rolls. There is no way to avoid these adverse social effects entirely, but they could be substantially alleviated at nominal cost if business were willing to make the effort.

For example, a company forced to close one of its plants could furnish the constituent community with a social impact analysis similar to the one proposed earlier for mergers, including a detailed explanation of its rationale for the shutdown. It could cooperate with the community to formulate a plan for eventually replacing the jobs lost; one option might be to use the empty plant to house newly created small businesses. Even if the plan resulted in the replacement of only a fraction of the jobs lost, the fact that the company had offered to help and had been open about its reasons for closing the plant would go a long way toward quelling the feelings of bitterness and hostility within the community. Incidentally, there would be more at stake here than good public relations: for every former employee who went back to work, the company would realize a savings in its unemployment costs.

A number of parallels can be drawn between plant closings and hostile mergers. Both wreak havoc on society to some extent. And both are garnering more and more attention from the public and the government alike. As noted earlier, some states have already moved to enact legislation pertaining to plant closings; it is logical to assume that similar restrictions will be placed on mergers sooner or later. If the rising public clamor against mergers doesn't result in constraints, the damage mergers cause by way of increasing unemployment certainly will. As unemployment and underemployment persist and become more widespread, the time will come when all reasonable effort will have to be made to preserve existing jobs and create new ones. Then, as always, society will overreact by imposing too-stringent controls.

The American business community must act now to promote and adopt policies on mergers, acquisitions, and plant closings that are responsive to society's needs. By voluntarily supporting the type of approach I am advocating—which would include new legislation to compel companies to behave more responsibly—we may be able to avoid further restrictions that would reduce the degree of operating freedom we presently enjoy.

There are those who contend that business is already overburdened with too many government regulations; my response is that more regulations are bound to come in any event. If we do not delay, if we are not afraid to join in the action, if we open our eyes to the danger, and if we cease being content to rely on business organizations that do little more than defend the status quo, we will be able to meet this challenge decisively, as we have met so many others in the past.

11

Corporate Policies and a New Business Culture

Much attention has been focused of late on the issues of corporate governance and corporate accountability. Spokesmen for the government, academia, labor, and business itself talk endlessly about ways to prevent the misuse of corporate power. Independent outside directors are deemed necessary to keep management on the straight and narrow, while inside directors are expected to function as little more than corporate cops. Security Exchange Commission regulations, laws requiring the greater public disclosure of the doings of private enterprise, modified laws of incorporation, legislation on overseas payments, audit committees, nominating committees, shareholder democracy, constituency representation—all hold center stage in what has fast become a complex and distracting theatrical production. It is complex in that there are no simple answers to the questions of how far business should be allowed to go and who should have the authority to

SOURCES

"Technology for Improving the Image of Business" address (also published as part of a technology booklet series), Minnesota Project on Corporate Responsibility Seminar, Long Lake, Minnesota, November 16, 1977.

"Technology and the Investor—Facing Up to Society's Urgent Problems" address (also published as part of a technology booklet series), National Investor Relations Conference, New York, New York, November 2, 1978.

"Technology and Corporate Governance" address (also published as part of a technology booklet series), Annual Meeting of the Minnesota Society of Certified Public Accountants, Bloomington, Minnesota, June 27, 1979.

"Innovation—The Longer Range View for Country and Company" address, President's meeting, Borg-Warner Corporation, Chicago, Illinois, September 26, 1980.

"Corporate Policies for Creating a New Business Culture" address, J. L. Kellogg Graduate School of Management, 30th Annual Fall Conference, Northwestern University, Evanston, Illinois, November 5, 1980.

"Technological Innovation and the Prudent Man" address (also published as part of a technology booklet series), General Mills Leadership Luncheon, Minneapolis, Minnesota, May 5, 1980; Mead Corporation, Cincinnati, Ohio, May 15, 1980; Harvard Business School Club, New York, New York, October 23, 1980.

decide; it is distracting in that it draws our attention away from the far more serious problems besetting our nation.

No one would argue with the assertion that surveillance and reasonable legislation are needed to correct deficiencies in the system. But surveillance and legislation alike can only relieve symptoms and effect cosmetic changes. What we really need is leadership in the form of industrial statesmen who are capable of using corporate power to solve society's major problems.

Leadership means action, not just talk. It is not enough to spend time in a seminar on improving productivity, or to attend a White House conference on balanced growth and economic planning, or to participate in studies on the role of business unless one takes the information gleaned from such an experience and puts it to use. Leadership also means the willingness to commit resources to programs aimed at meeting society's needs. Unfortunately, talk and studies are hallmarks of contemporary business culture in America while action and commitment are not. Few business leaders will accept the challenges and risks involved in adequately addressing our major social and economic problems. Few perceive the seriousness of the situation or understand that many of the old ways no longer suffice.

As I have maintained over the years, I am firmly convinced that technology can be effectively utilized to alleviate or eliminate the most pressing of the problems we are faced with today. I also believe that the impetus for solving these problems must come from business working in cooperation with other sectors of society. I am not suggesting that business should suddenly become altruistic; this would not do anyone any good in the long run. Rather, I am proposing that business take the reins in addressing society's needs because to do so makes good business sense.

The approach I am advocating is not based on theory, but on the results of the strategy Control Data adopted over a decade ago: namely, to turn unmet social and economic needs into profitable business opportunities, with an appropriate sharing of costs between business and government. In conformance with this strategy, we have initiated a wide variety of programs in the fields of education, small business assistance, rural development, urban renewal, and health care that have subsequently proved successful.

For example, our PLATO computer-based education and training system has been cost-effective in such diverse applications as vocational training and the teaching of basic skills; we expect that it will eventually extend into virtually all areas of education. Our Business and Technology Centers (BTCs) and Business Advisors, Inc. (BAI) are giving small businesses much needed assistance with financial planning, data processing, and technology transfer, along with various combinations of facilities and consulting services. Rural Ventures is showing that, with the proper selection and use of existing and emerging technologies, small family farms and food processors can make a significant contribution to the nation's food supply. City Venture is active in planning, initiating, and managing programs directed toward urban revitalization and renewal. Our StayWell and EAR programs are demonstrating that counseling services and health education delivered at the work site can measurably improve the physical and emotional well-being of employees and their families.

While murmurs of interest in the types of programs we offer have been heard in some corporate board rooms, the number of companies actually doing anything along similar lines remains discouragingly small. Despite the lack of a more meaningful response—the lack of action and commitment, in other words—I still feel that the fabric of American society could be vastly improved, and that business would find itself richly rewarded at the bottom line, if more companies were to follow our example.

The initiative to make this happen must come from the directors of the corporate boards of America. Equally important, directors must also move outside their own companies to generate support and establish cooperative relationships with others. Isolated programs will not do; nor will isolated instances of individual companies deciding to get involved or take a stand on a particular issue. What I am envisioning is no more and no less than the creation of a new business culture.

The old business culture—the one out of which most companies now operate—is characterized by an adversarial relationship between industry and government; an emphasis on low-risk, quick-payout investments; and a predilection for dwelling overlong on the subject of corporate governance and accountability. The primary task of most corporate directors is to monitor their companies' performance.

In the new business culture, corporate directors would embrace a new responsibility: that of catalyzing change by instituting a series of policies designed to stimulate innovation, encourage cooperation, and ensure that attention is paid to society's major unmet needs.

Innovation is crucial to progress and growth. Small businesses know this; they make their livings by being innovative. Most large corporations have forgotten how important innovation is, however, and are content with maintaining the status quo. A good policy to start with would be one that established a corporate atmosphere conducive to the development and adoption of two kinds of innovations: those required to keep the business profitable, and those that could be used to address society's unmet needs. In time, given proper guidance and informed decision making, the two would overlap and complement each other.

It would first be necessary to remove the formidable barrier to innovation present in most companies: specifically, the traditional pay system that is keyed to annual performance. This barrier could best be overcome by giving management the authority to propose additional expenditures for any and all urgently needed innovations. With the approval of the board, appropriate adjustments could then be made in executive bonus goals.

A semiannual review process could be implemented for the purpose of considering the company's needs for innovation and examining those innovations already under way. Part of this review process could be devoted to an evaluation of the more run-of-the-mill innovations aimed at improving existing products and services, but the primary emphasis would fall on those innovations related to major new offerings. Since the latter generally entail a greater degree of risk, higher costs, and completion dates that are difficult to estimate and subject to error, it would be essential to review them periodically so that budget adjustments could be made without penalizing executive bonuses.

It can be very difficult for a company to identify the need for a large-scale innovation, especially when the company has a history of success and its executives and directors are slow to recognize the warning signs of a coming setback. This was recently exemplified by General Motors, Ford, and Chrysler, where either the need for major innovations was not perceived or it was not given enough credence until trouble was on the doorstep. A policy requiring semiannual reviews might have cleared the way for innovations and helped the automobile industry to avert catastrophe.

A corporate policy on innovations in new fields could include the authorization of a special annual budget for innovations that would address societal needs, but would probably not be pursued as part of the company's mainstream business. This budget could be used to finance products and services requiring lengthy periods of development; those whose eventual outcomes were uncertain; and those whose markets either could not be estimated or appeared to be very small in comparison to the markets for existing offerings. Innovations in general should be protected from short-term contingencies; a separate budget could afford some measure of this protection. The rest could come from assigning control of innovative products to executives who were not responsible for overseeing the company's primary business.

Special emphasis could also be given to innovations that would help small companies and individuals outside the corporation. Every large company has extensive reserves of latent resources which, if used creatively, could not only add to its own profits, but also increase productivity nationwide and upgrade the lives of millions of people. By reaching outside its own walls, a company might well realize benefits *inside* those walls. Through the example set by the company, employees would be stimulated to think about change, be more amenable to change, and help to engender it.

In the new business culture, corporate directors would foster innovation and leave it room to thrive. To assemble and effectively utilize the wide variety of resources required for major innovations, they would also institute policies to encourage cooperation.

I have learned from experience that most executives do not at present think in these terms. To many, the idea of cooperation is anathema; they equate it with having to give away secrets or relinquish some of their own power. They will need time to get used to the idea. A relatively easy first step might involve participating in at least one consortium engaged in urban revitalization or rural development. Membership would require a modest investment and entail a relatively small degree of risk, and the benefits would be substantial. To begin with, participation would generate sales leads for the company's own products, since both urban and rural renewal lead to increased economic activity over a wide front. And the company would be among the first to discover potential markets for new products and services, since a revitalization effort usually makes use of the most advanced existing and emerging technologies.

Participation in a consortium would yield indirect benefits as well. For one, top company executives would be exposed to the range of human problems that exist in poverty-stricken areas. The enormity of these problems is almost impossible to grasp unless one either experiences them or sees them with one's own eyes. We have all read or heard about the riots in Miami, Orlando, and Chattanooga; we all know about the persistent and shockingly high unemployment rates among disadvantaged youth; we are all cognizant of the mushrooming crime statistics and the fact that millions of people are living at or below the poverty line. Yet few of us have been personally affected by the problems and frustrations that go hand-in-hand with being poor. If we continue to ignore them, however, we will be affected sooner or later. Our silence will generate even greater social unrest and disorder. And the time will come when we, too, are touched by the

The Plague of Violent Crime

They started walking at dusk, two teen-agers casually spreading the message that the streets of West Los Angeles were no longer safe. First they stopped Phillip Lerner and demanded money. Lerner had no cash, only his infant in a stroller. They let him pass and kept walking. They hailed Arkady and Rachel Muskin at a nearby intersection. The couple quickly handed over $8 and two wristwatches, and gratefully fled. Next the boys intercepted two elderly Chinese women and pulled out a pistol. When one woman tried to push the gun out of her face, four bullets blazed out, killing both. The boys kept walking. They came upon a trio of ▪▪▪ ▪▪▪ evening stroll. They took ▪▪▪ ▪▪▪ ▪▪▪ ▪▪▪ without

Defying any cure,
▪▪ overwhelms

can become a killing ground almost at whim. "Violent crime has been a very significant problem for a long time, particularly in the black community," says Los Angeles district attorney John Van de Kamp. "Now, because of the trespass of really horrible, senseless violence into places that were relatively sacrosanct, the white community realizes that no one is immune."

Is America caught in another crime wave? The answer depends on where you look. The standard statistical measure is the FBI Uniform Crime Reports, a compilation of offenses reported to the police. In 1979, after resting for several years at a high plateau, the rates of reported crime edged forward. But in 1980 they exploded. New York, Los Angeles, Miami and Dallas all showed record levels of murder, robbery and burglary. Detroit, which had been calming down since 1976 ▪▪▪ ▪▪ increases ▪▪▪

Murder is becoming commonplac▪

"It's not just us," said a man who had just heard that Pope John Paul II had been shot. "The whole world is crazy."

It was the sort of statement to be made quickly or not at all. It's not a point you like to dwell on. Too strong a case can be made.

Murder, the political and impersonal variety, has become commonplace. It is a condition of life, almost condoned — though not quite, not yet.

Murder is recognized as a useful, everyday, political tool, often little more than an attention-getting device.

Murderers now insist on recognition of their new status. A ▪

starves himself to death in Northern Ireland demanding the privileges of a political prisoner. Death the ultimate irrationality.

These group crimes, these political terrorists, meet the complexities of life with the simplicity of death. When their enemies are dead, they will negotiate with the neutral survivors.

And there are the lonely warped and maladjusted dictable These lone-- are stimulated ▪ political ▪- tional

Toll of Violence: 1.3 Million

The bullet that wounded ▪eagan made him a m▪ ▪ng list of Amer▪ ▪d by violen▪

OVERCROWDED PRISONS
Part of the Solution ▪ ... Or Part of ▪'

by SAM▪

"B
"Je▪
Pri▪
"She▪

As crim as an outra▪ manded stif▪ many of the ▪ tutes have bec▪ overcrowded. A tice Department ▪ thirds of the natio▪ now contain more they were designed cell built for a single ▪ now hold as many as ▪ mates.

At the same time, beca▪

Life Below the Poverty Line

Eighteen years ago this month Lyndon Baines Johnson took his war on poverty to Appalachia, one of the poorest regions in the richest nation of the world. In a frantic fifteen-hour swing through five states, LBJ—and Amer-ica—saw poverty at its worst. They saw it in the desperation of jobless mine workers in West Virginia. They saw it in the misery of sick, malnourished children in eastern Ken-tucky. And they saw it in Tom Fletcher, a 38-year-old sawmill worker. As he sat on the front porch of his three-room tar-papered shack near Inez, Ky. Fletcher told America through its President what it meant to stand in a family of eight—to survive year after year on the meager rations of charity and hope. For one day in the spring of 1964, the gaunt and tired face of Tom Fletcher was the symbol of poverty in America.

Today the face of poverty in America could belong to Joyce Reeves, 37, a stout, haggard di-vorcee who lives with her three children in a tiny trailer ▪▪rhead. Ky. Just ▪▪▪ ▪est of ▪

on dairy farms in southwestern Wisconsin. They are the "working poor" who toil as waitresses and day laborers and live on the edge. And they are the "new poor," a group pushed below the poverty line by a go-slow economy—and in danger of entering the "permanent poor," a growing group for whom the temporary crutch of welfare has turned into a straitjacket of lifelong depen-dency. They are a population on the dole. Michael—the walking wounded," says Michael Sheets, 28, who grew up poor in Appalachia. "casualties of a society trimming down."

Since 1964, when Lyndon Johnson signed the Economic Opportunity Act, America has spent hundreds of billions of dollars on the poor, a transfer of income that Martin Anderson, who resigned last month as Ronald Reagan's chief domestic policy adviser, calls "without precedent in the history of mankind." The money went to education and job training and to nutri-tion programs that have virtually eliminat-ed starvation and malnut▪ United States. Housing pr▪ and income supplement p▪ and ceased the plight of the el▪ ple say we threw mone▪ true," says Irwin Gar▪ and sociologist at th▪ consin. "We threw n▪ and it worked." ▪

High Cost: But ev▪ staunchest defend▪ its successes hav▪ programs were u▪ were ravaged by ▪ mise and unhea▪ levels of frau▪ some estimate▪ war on pov▪ directly re▪ logist Pie▪ pendenc▪ ▪ sag▪ ▪

A welfare mother in Philadelphia: Who's listening?

We are all cognizant of the mushrooming crime statistics and the fact that millions of people are living at or below the poverty line.

devastating consequences of escalating crime rates and must fear for our own safety and security.

Most corporate executives are not aware of how bad things really are. Some realize that the situation is quickly deteriorating and would like to do something about it, but they either do not know where to start or they lack sufficient influence to redirect corporate resources into socially meaningful channels. The consortium approach offers an answer that is gaining in credibility, and it is one I strongly recommend.

Cooperation should not be a matter of extracurricular activities alone. In the new business culture, corporations would also cooperate with one another and with the government. For example, a company might institute a policy requiring it to consider bringing out each new major product or service in cooperation with other companies. Admittedly, this idea conflicts with the concern for maintaining a proprietary position in the marketplace, but that concern is often specious because new technologies are so quickly diffused. This in turn leads to a widespread duplication of effort, which is not only costly and wasteful, but puts the United States at a competitive disadvantage. In other countries, cooperation among companies and between industry and government is far more common than in America, and the results are obvious.

What happens when companies do not cooperate is aptly illustrated by the case of our own computer industry. For the past 25 years, several firms have been duplicating one another's R&D and bringing out very similar products, and no single company has managed to secure that all-important proprietary position. Meanwhile, the Japanese have been steadily catching up to us. If we continue to refuse to cooperate, what happened to the automobile industry will happen to the computer industry; it is only a matter of time. At Control Data, we have participated in several joint efforts with other companies. These arrangements have benefited us handsomely and have never proved disadvantageous in any way.

Cooperation with the government is a somewhat stickier issue, primarily because the current government-business climate is so unhealthy. Business is weary of regulations and wants the government to leave it alone. Government officials are suspicious of business and mistrust its motives. The two are constantly at loggerheads, and neither seems willing to make the first move toward compromise and mutual understanding.

I believe that business should put aside its objections and make that move; there is little to lose and much to gain. Corporate directors could begin by requiring their companies to periodically assess areas in which cooperation seems possible. They could subsequently communicate better with the government during the planning stages of major new products and voice a willingness to consider and respond to public needs. The government could then provide financial support where appropriate and afford the company some measure of relief from onerous regulations.

In presenting my views of the new business culture, I have proposed that corporate directors play a far more active and incisive role than the one they are cast in at present. The question must now be raised as to who those directors should be. I am greatly disturbed by the tendency on the part of some corporations to populate their boards exclusively with independent outside directors, with the exception of the chairman. I feel that such a board is by nature incapable of adequately stimulating needed changes and innovations. To do so requires a high degree of personal commitment, the willingness to exercise initiative and share in the risks involved in implementing significant innovations, and the possession of a vast store of knowledge about a wide spectrum of technologies. I do not see how a board comprised entirely of outside directors can be expected to have these essential qualities. In my experience, the most desirable and effective board is one that is made up of both inside and outside directors—and there are times when a majority of insiders is preferable.

The much-touted word "independent" should be replaced by "competent." Thinking and speaking in terms of competence might help to eliminate the superficiality present in much of the current discourse on board composition, which is misleading to the public and could provoke misguided and stifling legislation on corporate governance.

Inept corporate governance is often cited as the reason why our economy is not growing at as fast a rate as the economies of other countries, most notably Japan and Germany. In my opinion, corporate governance as it exists in the United States today can better be described as unresponsive to economic and social realities.

A number of disparate plans have been proposed for the so-called "re-industrialization" of America, which has been widely publicized as the only thing that will save us. These plans suggest a variety of actions, ranging from tax incentives for increased business investment to a greater emphasis on the development of new sources of energy, the channeling of more investment moneys to industries having the greatest potential for growth, and a reduction in government regulations. About all that the various plans have in common is a noticeable lack of reference to national economic planning. This is a regrettable omission, because the need for economic planning is genuine and will be met in one way or another. Perhaps the final plan will stipulate little more than the dissemination of information and the practice of long-range planning; perhaps it will require the re-allocation of corporate resources under government direction and control. What ultimately happens will in many ways depend on our nation's corporate boards of directors.

We are at a crossroads: we can either choose to continue in our traditional mode of surveillance over the status quo, or we can provide the leadership needed to create a new business culture characterized by innovation and cooperation. We can sit back and wait and eventually find ourselves facing a hodgepodge of bureaucratically imposed national planning, or we can act like the industrial statesmen we are supposed to be. If we opt to behave as leaders, I am confident that together we will be able to revitalize American industry in an intelligent and democratic way.

William C. Norris, founder, chairman, and chief executive officer of Control Data Corporation, is a pioneer in the development of computer technology. He is also the architect of Control Data's business strategy of addressing society's major unmet needs as profitable opportunities.

Harold F. Williamson is professor emeritus of economics at Northwestern University, Evanston, Illinois.

James C. Worthy is professor of management, J.L. Kellogg Graduate School, at Northwestern University, Evanston, Illinois.